wal

Franco

Franco

Michael Streeter

HAUS PUBLISHING • LONDON

Originally published | blished in Great Britain in 2005 b
Haus Publishing Limited
26 Cadogan Court
London SW3 3BX

A CIP catalogue record for this book
is available from the British Library

ISBN 1-904950-32-9 (paperback)

Designed and typeset in Garamond
Printed and bound by Graphicom in Vicenza, Italy

Front cover: Arena
Back cover: Getty Images

www.hauspublishing.com

Contents

Life as a Soldier 1892 - 1926   1

First Taste of Politics 1926 - 1934   14

Joining the Plot 1935 - 1936   26

Taking Control 1936 - 1937   37

Total victory   51

Peace but no Reconciliation 1939 - 1940   65

Staying Out of the War 1940 - 45   80

Alone 1946 -1953   95

In From the Cold 1953 - 1962   107

A Dying Regime 1964 - 1975   122

Endnotes   136

Further Reading   140

Picture Sources   141

Chronology   142

Index   156

Life as a Soldier 1892–1926

The arrival of Francisco Franco Bahamonde into the world on 4 December 1892 was an uneventful affair. Born in the early hours, Francisco was the second son of Nicolás Franco Salgado-Araujo and Pilar Bahamonde y Pardo de Andrade. After the eldest son Nicolás and Francisco came another boy, Ramón, followed by Pilar and later another daughter Paz who died as a child.

The community into which Francisco was born also seemed an ordinary, uneventful kind of place. El Ferrol was a small naval base in Galicia, tucked away in the far top left corner of Spain. Removed from the cosmopolitan influences of Barcelona or Madrid, it was an isolated town in a remote part of the country, dominated by the sea and its beautiful if sometimes desolate coastline. Yet the influence of both his family and his surroundings were to have a crucial impact on the young Francisco and on his path to becoming Spain's dictator for 36 years.

The marriage of Franco's parents was an unhappy one, and their fundamental differences of character and eventual split played a part in shaping both the man and his politics. His father Nicolás Franco came from a family with a long tradition of service in the Spanish Navy, though in the administrative section rather than the sea-going part. This was a crucial distinction in a society very aware of status, and meant that the Franco family was not part of the elite social set of El Ferrol. They were reasonably comfortably off, however, and Nicolás eventually rose to a senior position equivalent in rank to that of a lower-level general. He was also an outgoing, womanising, pleasure-seeking man whose politics matched his personality. Nicolás was opinionated, generally anti-clerical, had sympathies with freemasonry and was broadly liberal in his outlook. This liberalism stopped, however, the moment he crossed the threshold of the family's modest house on the Calle de Maria in El Ferrol where he was a strict disciplinarian.

The contrast between Nicolás and his wife, whose own father was a naval commander, could hardly have been more striking. Ten years younger than her husband, Pilar was slim, pretty, self-effacing, undemonstrative and conservative in her outlook on life and in her politics. She was also a deeply pious Catholic. Their marriage in 1890, when Pilar aged 24, was probably doomed from the start. Out of the three sons, it was Francisco who inherited his mother's personality traits while his brothers more resembled their father. Francisco was his mother's favourite but never seemed to win his father's love or approval – not even when he eventually became ruler of Spain.

From an early age Francisco – often known by the nickname 'Paquito' a common diminutive meaning 'little Frank' – was a very serious boy, curiously aloof and emotionally detached, though with a stubborn determination to get his own way. When he was just eight years old, his sister Pilar held a red-hot needle into his wrist. The boy's only reaction was to observe *how shocking the way burnt flesh smells*.[1] It was an early glimpse of the glacial coldness that Franco often displayed later in life, a trait that caused people to fear him. At the same time the adult Franco could be intensely sentimental and on occasions would cry for the slightest of reasons, while affecting cool indifference at times of bad news or emotional loss. This odd alternation between coldness and sentimentality was to be a key feature of Franco's personality.

Another reason for the young Franco's withdrawn personality was his physical appearance and other people's reactions to it. He was a small and thin child who would never grow above 5ft 4ins tall and whose nose, ears and deep brown eyes seemed too big for his head. His voice was high-pitched and unimpressive and also much-mocked.

Neither his physique or his personality seemed to mark out Franco for an illustrious career in the armed services, yet from an early age he was determined to have just that. In fact, in a small naval town such as El Ferrol, joining the military was considered just about the only way to have a decent career. Franco's first choice was to join the Navy, either in administration like his father or ideally in the sea-faring branch. So in 1905, aged just 12,

Francisco was sent to the Naval Preparatory School in the town to get him ready for joining the Navy. His older brother Nicolás had already joined the school, as had his cousin Pacón or 'big Frank'. Pacón was to remain a loyal companion and servant of Franco for the rest of his life.

Yet Franco's dreams of a great naval career – and perhaps of outdoing his father – were shattered. The Naval Academy – the next step for would-be naval officers – closed its doors to new entrants as part of a series of government cutbacks. For the 14-year-old it was a very personal demonstration of the fluctuating fortunes of the military at the hands of civilian government. Already Franco was very well aware of the Spanish military's shattering defeat at the hands of the United States in 1898 over Cuba, Spain's last great stronghold in Latin America.

Though Franco was not even six at the time of this humiliation, the impact it had on a naval base such as El Ferrol was immense. No one growing up there could fail to be influenced by it. The army and navy saw this military disaster as a symbol of how corrupt, ineffectual and unpatriotic civilian government had betrayed the armed forces by sending them into battle with poor equipment and preparation. Franco shared this view.

After the loss of most of Spain's colonies in the early 19th century, Cuba remained her most coveted Latin American possession. Yet corrupt and inept government led to a fierce independence movement, led by José Martí 1853-1895. The United States government and public supported Cuba's independence and after the US warship Maine mysteriously blew up in early 1898 the increasing tensions led to war. The Spanish-American War lasted just three months in which the US navy sank Spain's ageing fleet and US troops quickly secured the island. Spain lost not just Cuba but Puerto Rico and the Philippines.

If the glamour of the navy was now closed to Franco, then the next best option was the army. In August 1907 therefore, having passed his entrance exams, he arrived at the Military Academy in Toledo to start his career as an officer in the Spanish army.

It was to prove a momentous year for the 14-year-old. Not only was he joining the harsh environment of an army institution and was living away from home for the first time, but home life itself was also to change irrevocably. Franco's father had taken up new postings in Cadiz and then Madrid, while his mother Pilar stayed at the family home in El Ferrol. It was the effective end of the marriage. The split affected Pilar Bahamonde deeply. Not only did she feel betrayed as a woman – Nicolas soon set up home with someone else in the capital – the breaking of their marriage vows offended her religious principles and brought scandal upon her family. The young Franco was aware of his mother's anguish and undoubtedly also felt betrayed by his father. Already he was conscious of the profound difference between the free–thinking, free–living liberalism of his father and the pious Catholic conservatism of his mother. Soon he would come to believe that the values reflected by his father were bad not just for his family, but for the whole of Spain too. It was a view reinforced and shaped by the military world he was now about to enter.

Toledo, which lies south west of Madrid, is not just hundreds of miles from El Ferrol, it also has a very different geography and climate. In contrast to Galicia's green lands and relatively temperate weather, inland Toledo is hot, dry and dusty in the summer and often bitterly cold in the winter. In many ways it feels like a completely different Spain. But it was not just a dramatic change of scene the teenage Franco had to cope with. The young cadets were subjugated to the full and often complex demands of Spanish Army discipline, under which even to wear the wrong item of uniform in the wrong part of the Academy could lead to punishment. The emphasis in the Academy was on the need to obey orders, the importance of individual bravery, absolute loyalty to the Fatherland and the crucial role of the army in Spain rather than on new techniques of warfare. The young cadet also had to endure taunts at his expense, not just because of his height and voice, though these were mocked – and his instructors did not help either by insisting that he drilled with a specially shortened rifle. He was also teased because of his serious nature. Unlike most of the other cadets, for example, Franco did not take part in regular womanising exploits in Toledo.

Yet the stubborn side of Franco's character meant that he would not long tolerate being bullied. When he got into trouble because his books had been hidden, Franco threw a candlestick at an older cadet's head and provoked a fight. Later, when asked by officers to reveal the names of his tormentors, Franco defiantly refused. Though he was never a popular cadet, such behaviour at least won him a grudging respect from his fellow students. These included such men as Juan Yague and Camilo Alonso Vega who would feature prominently in Franco's future career.

Despite the problems, Franco threw himself into army life with some gusto. At the Academy all were equal before the discipline of the army and this ultimately helped him overcome his difficulties. The cadet seemed to find comfort in the routine of army life and its emphasis on the past glories of Spain. Yet if Franco had taken well to military life it was not yet reflected in his achievements. When in July 1910, having completed his training, he was commissioned as a second lieutenant, Franco was placed just 251st out of the 312 cadets who finished the course.

It was a modest start for a future military hero and for the next two years the new officer and his fellow Academy member Pacón had little opportunity to enhance their status. They were both posted to garrison duty with a small regiment back in El Ferrol, having been ruled too junior to serve in Africa. Back in

In 1904 France agreed to grant northern Morocco to Spain, who already had enclaves in Africa at Ceuta since 1640 and Melilla since 1556. This new territory, known as Spanish Marocco and which formally became a Spanish Protectorate in 1912, was of debatable economic value and its Rif tribes people were extremely hard to police. Yet it satisfied the needs of those on the right who wanted an empire. However, many on the left considered the project a waste of time, money and above all the lives of working men. The territory became part of an independent Morocco in 1956.

his home town Franco could at least be close to his unhappy mother, and had time to develop shy crushes on friends of his sister Pilar. But it was in Africa that Francisco Franco wanted to be, and where, unlike on the Peninsula, a young officer could rise quickly through the ranks through bravery in combat. Early in 1912 the 19-year-old officer got his wish.

The Spanish Protectorate in Africa was always a divisive issue. In 1909 the Conservative government ordered an ill-judged military incursion into the territory to protect Spanish mining rights. The result was protests and strikes in Barcelona where reservists were called up to fight in Africa. The demonstrations and attacks were not just anti-military, but anti-clerical too for the Church was seen as an ally of the hated ruling elite. The subsequent ruthless government quashing of the unrest led to hundreds of dead and wounded and saw up to 2,000 arrests. This brief but intense period of unrest became known as the 'tragic week' (*semana trágica*). Although at the time Franco was far away at the Academy in Toledo, he and his fellow cadets followed the events with intense interest. It reinforced the belief of him and many others in the military that the government was inept and that the Fatherland was at risk from dangerous revolutionary forces.

Yet when Franco arrived in the ramshackle colonial town of Melilla in February 1912 it was not politics that excited him but the hope of seeing action and of advancing his career. During the next fourteen years, most of them spent in Africa, he was to achieve both goals spectacularly. If his childhood and the Academy in Toledo had helped prepare the way for the adult Franco, it was in Africa that his character and beliefs were really forged. Though he never bothered to learn Arabic and showed little interest in local customs, there is a sense in which Morocco – or at least his life as a soldier there – entered Franco's soul. In 1938 Franco himself claimed that *without Africa I can scarcely explain myself to myself, nor can I explain myself properly to my comrades in arms.*[2] This was a time when, freed from the shackles of peninsula life, Franco was able to reinvent himself. Gone, or at least partially suppressed, was the awkward and reserved youth, and in its place emerged a dashing and utterly ruthless war hero. As a child he had played games of heroes and villains in which he had playacted the role of heroic characters. In Africa Franco had the chance to become one.

In June 1912 Franco received his first and only promotion due to seniority when he was made a first lieutenant. All his other steps up the military ladder would be earned by merit. Early the next year Franco applied to join the

Francisco Franco as a young man. c1920

native police, known as the *Regulares*. The native police troops were tough Moroccan mercenaries with a fierce reputation. Curiously the awkward looking young officer from Galicia seemed to revel in leading these troops and soon carved out a reputation for personal bravery and bold leadership.

Based at Tetuán, Franco led his mercenaries in a number of engagements against Moroccan guerrillas, including one in September that earned him a Military Merit Cross, first class. Then in February 1914 he was promoted to captain for his bravery and leadership in battle. One of Franco's attributes was his coolness under fire. Indeed he was almost reckless in the way he ignored enemy bullets whizzing around him during battle.

His recklessness was exemplified by Franco's insistence on riding a white horse when commanding troops in battle. It was as if the young officer was testing his own invincibility, and the more dangerous situations he survived the more he came to feel that he was a man with a mission. It was at this time that Franco, who had temporarily abandoned the piety of his youth, gained his reputation as a man who was 'without fear, women or masses' *('sin miedo, sin mujeres y sin misa')*.[3] His Moroccan troops certainly felt there was something different about Franco, and believed his invulnerability was due to *baraka*, a mixture of divine protection and good fortune.

This luck held good even when, on 29 June 1916, he was shot in the stomach during a successful assault on a guerrilla stronghold at El Biutz between Ceuta and Tetuán. Though Spain stayed out of the First World War, its army nevertheless suffered heavy casualties in Africa. Nearly 17,000 officers and soldiers died during the time of Franco's service in Africa, a significant number of them from stomach wounds. Yet despite the worst fears of his senior officers, the stubborn Franco clung to life. The bullet had narrowly missed any vital organ and soon he was to make a full recovery. It was the only injury Franco sustained in more than a decade of active service in Africa; he was still protected by *baraka*.

Franco's bravery at El Biutz led to several important outcomes. First, he was recommended for promotion to the rank of major and for Spain's highest bravery medal, the Gran Cruz de San Fernando. When the Ministry of War blocked both, an outraged Franco took the unusual step of directly appealing to King Alfonso XIII who was Commander-in-Chief of the army. Eventually the wounded officer was granted his promotion though still denied his medal. The episode showed Franco's idea of his own worth and also his determination to fight for what he believed was rightfully his.

Ironically, his promotion to major led to Franco being posted back to the peninsula, this time to Oviedo in Asturias. It was here, during an otherwise uneventful posting, that Franco met and fell for his future wife María del Carmen Polo y Martínez Valdés. When they first met Carmen Polo was just 15 and still a convent schoolgirl. She came from a well-connected local family, was a devout Catholic and was slim and elegant. In some respects, therefore, she was similar to Franco's mother Pilar though she was to prove a much more forceful character. The 24-year-old Franco pursued Carmen with his usual determination, refusing to be put off by her family's disapproval of the match on the grounds of his modest background and hazardous occupation.

Franco had shown an interest in girls from an early age, and there is no evidence to support Army rumours that he was homosexual. Equally it was true that the reserved Franco did not seem much interested in sex. Some people believed that his lack of interest stemmed from his abdominal injury and that it may have affected his sexual prowess. However, Franco's abstention from sexual adventures was exhibited well before the 1916 injury, and probably stemmed from disapproval of his father's many amorous exploits.

The African veteran José Millán Astray was a soldier of legendary bravery who had many wounds to prove it. Though his idea for a Spanish Foreign Legion was modelled on the famous French version, he effectively moulded it into an extension of his own personality. His recruits were criminals, social outcasts and foreign malcontents, and Millán called them the 'bridegrooms of death' ('los novios de la muerte'), encouraging them to revel in death. They quickly gained a reputation not only for bravery but also savagery, and committed many atrocities against Moroccan fighters and civilians.

While Franco was in the middle of his six-year-long courtship of Carmen, another important consequence of his wound and subsequent promotion occurred. At a sharp–shooting course in 1918 he met Major José Millán Astray.

The colourful Millán Astray was a fellow Africa veteran – or *Africanista* as they were known - and as such he and Franco shared similar views about

The future General Franco addressing his troops in Spanish Morocco

the role of the military, Africa and civilian government. Thus when in 1920 Millán Astray finally got the go-ahead for his idea of a Spanish Foreign Legion, he asked the youthful Major Franco to be his second-in-command. For a moment Franco wavered. Carmen Polo had just agreed to marry him and taking up the post would mean delaying their wedding. Yet the lure of Africa won, and by October that same year he was back in Africa. A saddened Carmen later revealed her reaction to Franco's departure: 'The first tears that I shed as a woman were for him.'[4]

Back in Africa the 27-year-old Franco revelled in his new role. From the start he showed an absolute ruthlessness with the unruly men under his command. Even the smallest breach of discipline resulted in severe penalties. When a disgruntled legionnaire had thrown his inedible food into the face of an officer Franco ordered him to be shot on the spot. The other troops were then ordered to march past the body of their dead colleague. On another occasion a visiting colleague from Toledo days gently remonstrated with Franco over his decision to have two deserters shot. *You don't realise what kind of people they are*, replied Franco. *If I didn't act with an iron hand this would soon be chaos*.[5]

Yet if the men were expected to show absolute discipline within camp, Millán Astray and Franco gave them license to brutalise the enemy and the local population. They routinely took enemy heads as 'trophies'. On one occasion legionnaires sent a basket of flowers to an aristocratic Spanish woman who had helped organise a team of nurses. Garnishing the flowers were the heads of two Moroccans. It is a debatable point whether Franco's time in Africa brutalised him and made him apparently indifferent to such savagery, or whether the introspective young man was already able to detach himself from barbaric behaviour – which he rarely took part in himself. Either way, in later life Franco showed that he had absorbed the lesson of how terror tactics can cow the enemy into submission.

Despite their barbaric reputation, the Foreign Legion did have a more conventional function, none more so than in July 1921 when another military disaster befell the Spanish Army. An apparently pointless advance west of Melilla had led to a massacre of Spanish troops near the village of Annual and the loss of miles of territory to the local Berber tribes. Franco and his men were dispatched to sort out the mess. Once again he showed himself to be a skilled as well as brave battlefield commander as he and his men repulsed the enemy.

Over the next few months the exploits of the legion and in particular its dashing young major began to attract appreciative press comment in Spain. There was great excitement over an incident in early 1922 when Franco and his entire unit were ordered to rescue a group of soldiers who were under attack. Franco insisted that just 12 men were necessary, called for volunteers, and hurried off with them. The next day they returned with the heads of 12 tribesmen. Franco's public reputation rose even higher when in 1922 he published his exploits in his *Diary of a Battalion* (*Diario de una bandera*). In the same year Franco, who had taken over temporary command of the Legion after Millán had suffered yet another injury, was presented to Alfonso XIII. The king generously praised his courage. With a modesty typical of Franco at the time, but certainly not of later years, he told the press: *What he has said about me is a bit exaggerated. I merely fulfil my duty.* Franco instead praised the bravery of his men. *You could go anywhere with them*, he insisted.[6] The young officer's heroic profile was growing by the day.

Franco's relentless upwards march was briefly checked when, for a variety of reasons, Millán stood down as head of the Legion. The 30-year-old major, who was deemed too junior for the commanding officer role, was immediately granted a transfer back to Oviedo, where at last he could plan his delayed wedding to Carmen. However her joy was short-lived. When Millán's replacement was killed in action, Franco was promoted in June to lieutenant colonel and made commanding officer of the Foreign Legion. Soon he was back in Africa and back in the thick of the action.

While Franco returned to Africa the political situation in Spain was becoming unstable. Once again Spain's involvement in Morocco was a crucial and divisive issue. In particular there was growing tension over the ongoing inquiry into the disaster at Annual. Amid mounting disorder – though the country was by no means out of control – General Miguel Primo de Rivera staged a coup on 13 September 1923 and seized power as military dictator, while the king remained Head of State. Franco was not involved in the plot though he did not oppose it. Like many *Africanistas*, however, he was concerned about Primo's lukewarm commitment to Spanish military presence in Morocco.

Franco, however, had other matters on his mind as on 23 October he and Carmen finally married in Oviedo. It was a lavish and very public event, with the local military governor representing Alfonso XIII as the official best man to Lieutenant-Colonel Franco. The press lapped up the occasion. At last the noble military hero, who had delayed his wedding to serve his country in dangerous missions in Africa, was able to claim his bride. One newspaper even referred to the 'wedding of an heroic Caudillo'. *Caudillo* is a Spanish name meaning 'warrior leader' and carries echoes of great soldier leaders from Spain's past and was used for fighters who led the fight against Roman occupation. One day Franco would claim that title for real.

Franco and Carmen had a strong relationship. Though it seems never have to been very passionate, the marriage gave Franco a degree of emotional security. Carmen was fiercely loyal to and also ambitious for her husband, while her piety also influenced him. Over the years she became a powerful influence on Francoism. In fact the German propaganda chief Josef Goebbels would later complain that Franco allowed Spain to be 'practically governed not by himself but by his wife and her father confessor'.[7]

Franco's time in Africa was drawing to a close but he still had time to continue his astonishing rise through the ranks. In February 1925 the 32-year-old was promoted to full Colonel and in September of that year he led the Legion as part of a huge Franco-Spanish attempt to stamp out rebellion in Morocco. The Spanish contingent landed at the bay of Alhucemas, west of Melilla. The attack nearly stalled at the start and indeed the order was given for the invasion force to retreat. However Franco, who was leading the first troops on the beach, audaciously chose to countermand the order. Under heavy fire he and his men waded ashore and eventually managed to stage a bridgehead. As a result the invasion and the whole campaign was a success.

Franco's reward for his exploits at Alhucemas – the success of the venture helped ensure his disobedience of an order was overlooked – was more gushing publicity and yet another promotion. On 3 February 1926 he became a brigadier general, making him at 33 probably the youngest general in Europe at the time. It was an astonishing achievement for a soldier who had finished 251st in his class 16 years earlier. The promotion to general also meant that there was now no position for him in Morocco. Yet while Franco was obliged to leave Africa, his experiences as an *Africanista* were never to leave him. They underpinned his beliefs and actions as his career took a new and more political turn.

First Taste of Politics 1926-1934

When he returned to the mainland Brigadier General Franco was given the prestigious command of the First Brigade of the First Division of the army, stationed in Madrid. It was not the most taxing of positions and from the start Franco showed a willingness to delegate to his officers, a habit he would increasingly adopt in his career. Slowly, too, Franco's image began to change. In Africa he had been a man of action, a dashing war hero prepared to act boldly. From now on, however, Franco started to show a reluctance to commit himself to a decision until he had fully weighed up all the consequences. Occasionally the boldness of his Africa days would re-emerge, such as when he seized the initiative at the start of the Civil War in 1936. For the most part, however, his prudence prevailed.

Franco also developed his considerable political skills at this time. Both before and after he assumed power in Spain, Franco was usually successful in convincing competing parties that he was really on their side. He was a master of the cryptic remark and of convoluted statements that could be understood in different ways. In this sense he was true to his roots. Galicians or gallegos are noted for their craftiness and in Spanish an ambiguous statement is known as a *galleguismo*. An example of the contradictions in Franco's personality was shown back in 1924 when as commander of the Foreign Legion he had played host to the new dictator General Primo. At the time Primo was considering a withdrawal from Morocco, much to the chagrin of the Legion and other *Africanistas*. Franco gave a speech attacking the idea of abandoning Africa, while his junior officers hissed General Primo's remarks. Later, however, a worried Franco anxiously sought out the dictator to clarify his position. The ambitious Franco had learnt the importance of keeping in with authority to further his own career.

Despite the 1924 incident, Franco had good reason to be grateful for the dictatorship of General Primo. On the surface at least the regime had restored a degree of calm to Spain and for a while delivered near full employment.

Ramón Franco

On a personal level Franco had plenty to be happy about as well. His hometown of El Ferrol had staged lavish celebrations to mark his military exploits, and those of his aviator brother Ramón, who on 3 February 1926 had daringly flown across the South Atlantic. Indeed, 12 February 1926 was declared a local holiday in their honour. Then on 14 September Carmen gave birth to a daughter, also called Carmen though she was often known as 'Nenuca'. She was Franco's only child.

There have been suggestions that Nenuca was not the couple's daughter but was instead the adopted offspring of one of Ramón's many affairs. However the only 'evidence' for this is that there are no photographs of Carmen Polo showing her pregnant, and there is no serious reason to suppose that Nenuca was not Franco's child. Certainly Franco genuinely loved her and commented: *When Carmen was born I thought I would go mad with joy.*[8]

Soon Franco's career was moving upwards again. When as part of military reforms General Primo proposed a new combined General Military Academy at Zaragoza, he chose Franco to be its first Director. Partly this was because of Franco's

When General Miguel Primo de Rivera y Orbaneja (1870-1930) staged his coup on 13 September 1923 it was greeted with relief by many parts of society. Since 1876 Spain had been governed by alternate Conservative and Liberal civilian administrations who had presided over unrest, corruption and deepening divisions in society. Many felt that Spain was in need of 'regeneration'. But though Primo's regime had some early success, ultimately the naturally conservative dictator was unable to satisfy either the Left, Right or even all the military, and amid growing opposition stepped down on 30 January 1930.

Primo de Rivera and King Alfonso XIII with members of de Rivera's cabinet

rising status, and partly because Franco had shown no inclination to join the coterie of disgruntled officers who were scheming against Primo. The head of the new Academy was an important and influential position, for it gave Franco the chance to influence the minds of a whole new generation of officers. Many of its instructors were fellow *Africanistas*, ensuring that the cadets were left in no doubt both of the importance of the army and of the inherent weaknesses of democratic civilian governments.

Though Franco had a wealth of experience of battle from Africa, he was no military strategist. The colonial war in which he had fought was a relatively primitive one involving the slow painstaking seizing of territory and personal acts of bravery and boldness. Franco knew little of emerging modes of warfare. This would be reflected in his later conduct of the Civil War. Meanwhile, though new techniques were taught at the Academy, the emphasis was put on moral and military virtues such as patriotism, valour, blind obedience to discipline and loyalty to the monarch. The 'ten commandments' that Franco set out for the Academy when it opened its doors in October 1928 reflect this. They included: loving the fatherland and king, showing military spirit in vocation and discipline, showing the qualities of a gentleman and protecting one's reputation, fulfilling duties to the letter and volunteering for sacrifice at times of greatest risk.[9]

During his time at the Academy Franco gained a reputation for discipline that reached all areas of the cadets' lives. Curiously, the general would even pounce on unsuspecting cadets in the city and demand to see whether they were carrying condoms as required as part of his drive against venereal disease. The provincial life also suited Franco better than Madrid, where he had never felt at ease in high society. Here in Zaragoza the leading local families feted the heroic military figure who had come into their midst. The flattering attention fed Franco's growing sense of self-importance at a time when, as Primo's dictatorship foundered, there was a sense of impending crisis.

The Bourbon King Alfonso XIII (1886 – 1941) was the posthumous son of Alfonso XII and was declared king upon his birth. His mother Queen Maria Christina was regent until Alfonso was 16 in 1902. Alfonso married Princess Victoria Eugénie of Battenberg, granddaughter of Queen Victoria, in 1906, though the day was marred by an attempt to assassinate the couple. Alfonso's support for Primo de Rivera's dictatorship fatally undermined his status as a constitutional monarch. In April 1931, aware that he no longer had the support even of all the army, Alfonso left Spain, though he did not formally abdicate.

The feeling that serious change was imminent did not vanish when General Primo left power in early 1930 and went into self-imposed exile in Paris. For many in Spain, there still remained the issue of King Alfonso XIII himself.

The growing unpopularity of Alfonso had led to a resulting increase in Republicanism, even among sections of the armed forces. To Franco's acute embarrassment, one of those who fell in with the Republican cause was his

younger brother. Ramón, who was implicated in a plot to overthrow the monarchy, was thrown into a military prison, escaped and then fled abroad. Franco wrote to his younger brother begging him to give up his support for armed insurrection. In a letter that makes interesting reading in the light of later events, Franco wrote: *Any extremist and violent revolution will drag (the Fatherland) down to the most hateful of tyrannies.*[10]

Soon Franco had to intervene more directly in the growing political

A triumphant General Franco returns to Zaragoza

crisis. On 12 December 1930 a group of junior officers staged an uprising at Jaca, north of Zaragoza. It was meant to be co-ordinated with a general strike, but the officers had acted too early. Their rebellion was quickly put down and the two leaders shot, though not before Franco had armed his cadets and dispatched them to block the road between Jaca and Zaragoza.

Despite such incidents, the loyalist Franco still did not realise that Alfonso and the monarchy were in peril. Perhaps he could not take the threat seriously because of the bizarre actions of his Republican brother. On 15 December 1930 Ramón, who was still on the run, flew an aircraft over the royal palace in Madrid, intending to bomb it. He apparently only held back after spotting women and children in the palace grounds and so instead dropped leaflets urging a general strike. Revealingly, Franco was more concerned that some retaliatory leaflets dropped shortly afterwards had described his brother as a 'bastard'. The Academy Director even travelled to Madrid to seek reassurances that this slur on his family name was not inspired by the Government.

A test of the monarchy's popularity came in local elections in April 1931. Although the monarchists – for whom Franco voted – came top in the first round, the second round showed huge support for Republican candidates, especially in the cities. Alfonso's already precarious position was made worse when the head of the Civil Guard General José Sanjujro told the government he could not guarantee the loyalty of his men. On 14 April Alfonso XIII felt he had little choice but to stand aside to avoid, as he put it, a 'fratricidal civil war'.[11] Briefly Franco considered marching on Madrid with his cadets in support of the king, but his prudence and conversations with fellow officers made him hold back. Years later Franco was scornful of those in power for, as he put it, *handing [the monarchy] over to the revolutionaries without firing a single shot in defence of legality.*[12] For the time being, however, a shocked Franco had to get used to living in a Republican Spain.

Franco's deep dislike for the Republic was a typical though by no means universal view among senior army officers. He was by nature conservative, pro-monarchy and, after a brief lapse, a faithful Catholic. Therefore the three main areas the new government wanted to reform – the Church, access to land and the military – were almost bound to alarm Franco. Franco hated, too, the idea of greater autonomy for regions such as Catalonia and the Basque country as this he felt undermined the unity of the Fatherland. He also feared the Republic was a harbinger of communism and since 1928 had subscribed to a Geneva-based journal that warned of the threat from international Marxist-Leninism.

Now these were not Franco's only fears. He was for example convinced that freemasonry threatened Spain. This particular antipathy probably had personal roots. His father had been sympathetic to freemasonry and his brother Ramón was a member, while it seems that Franco's application to join the masons was rejected 'on three separate occasions'.[13] Franco came to associate freemasonry with atheism, liberalism and democracy and with France, Britain and the United States. Yet many army officers were masons too, and more significantly many were also Republicans. These included the prominent general Gonzalo Queipo de Llano.

In his response to the Second Republic, Franco faced a dilemma. He was fearful it would pave the way for a communist takeover of Spain. Yet Franco's natural inclination as a soldier was to obey his country's government, and more importantly he was unwilling to do anything that would seriously damage his career. Thus his initial reaction was one of grudging acceptance of his new Republican masters while at the same time making it clear that he disapproved of them. On 15 April he told his cadets that the Army was *obliged, with serenity and unity, to sacrifice its thoughts and its ideology for the good of the nation and the tranquillity of the Patria (Fatherland).*[14] However Franco rather pedantically and pointedly refused to hoist the new Republican flag at the Academy until he had received a written order.

Many in the military were soon angered by measures planned by the

Spain's First Republic had been created in 1873 and had lasted just a year. However growing disenchantment with Alfonso XIII and especially his support for a military dictatorship led to a broad-based opposition to the monarch and support for a republic. This included mainly middle class Republican radicals of the left and right, Basques and Catalans who sought autonomy, socialists and even disaffected monarchists. Representatives had signed a pact in San Sebastian to establish a provisional government once the monarchy fell. It survived from 1931 – 1936, and ultimately failed to satisfy supporters on the centre left while simultaneously alienating the forces of the right.

new Minister of War, Manuel Azaña. He was probably the most talented member of the government and wanted to modernise and de-politicise the military. These changes included massive voluntary retirements (though on full pay), the punishment of those responsible for executing the rebels of Jaca, a review of the promotions of officers who had received them on merit – mostly the *Africanistas* – and the need to swear loyalty to the Republic. These were deeply divisive issues. For example the army had long been split between those who supported promotion by merit, and those who insisted it be based on length of service. Franco and the *Africanistas* fell firmly in the former camp.

However, though Franco was deeply dismayed by such matters, his real wrath was reserved for a reform that most directly affected him, Azaña's decision to close the Academy in Zaragoza. Franco was rarely able to separate the personal from the political. He saw the decision as a personal attack on him by Azaña and a small coterie of Republican military officers – dubbed the 'black cabinet' by some – who advised the minister. Without intending to, Azaña had made an implacable enemy. In a farewell speech to cadets Franco attacked an alleged favouritism shown towards Republican officers. He also pointedly remarked that the toughest part of discipline lay in accepting orders from above *when one knows that higher authority is in error and acting out of hand.*[15] Later, in private with Pacón, Franco broke down in tears. The general's reward for this clear display of dissent was an official reprimand, the first on his hitherto unblemished record. This added to his already burning resentment of the Second Republic in general and Azaña in particular.

The second half of 1931 was undoubtedly a low point in a career that had known remarkably few setbacks. Franco languished without a posting on 80 per cent pay back at Carmen's house in Oviedo, from where the couple looked out with increasing bitterness on events on Spain. Franco and his devout wife had already been appalled in May when anarchists in Madrid, Seville and other cities had torched churches. Franco later stated that these burnings profoundly influenced his view of the Second Republic.[16]

Azaña, who now saw Franco as the main threat in the event of any military uprising, and who briefly had him under surveillance, finally gave the general a chance of rehabilitating himself with the Republic in February 1932. The command of an infantry brigade in La Coruña was hardly a prestigious position. But the posting saved the inactive general from being forcibly retired and also meant that Franco could be close to his ageing mother. However, he felt no hint of gratitude towards the minister he already blamed for trying to wreck his career.

Even now, however, despite the resentment that the general felt towards the regime, he was not willing to throw himself into any plot against it. This was partly because he felt that the situation in Spain, though bad, was not yet out of control. It was also because the cautious Franco did not believe any coup yet had enough military support to succeed. Instead it was left to another *Africanista* General José Sanjurjo, currently the head of the Civil Guard, to lead the way.

In December 1931 a group of landless labourers – one of Spain's poorest and most wretched groups of workers – had staged a peaceful protest in the remote Extremaduran village of Castilblanco. Four Civil Guards opened fire and killed one of the protestors, whose enraged colleagues then hacked and beat the four military policemen to death. The Left was appalled at the deaths of innocent protestors, the Right equally incandescent at the attack on the forces of law and order for which they blamed the government. Sanjurjo was eventually removed from his position. Almost immediately the so-called 'Lion of the Rif' became the focal point of a plot against the regime.

However, when Sanjurjo launched the coup on 10 August 1932 it was a damp squib and attracted little support. Franco had known about it in advance but despite some typically ambiguous comments to its supporters, had ultimately made it clear he wanted no involvement. Partly this was because of his dislike of Sanjurjo whom he blamed for the downfall of the monarchy.

Franco's non–involvement was in hindsight a shrew move. On the Right people came round to his view that for a coup to succeed it had to be very well prepared, much better supported and ideally have the backing of the Civil Guard. Meanwhile Azaña, who was relieved to learn that Franco remained at his post during the coup attempt, believed the general was now fully rehabilitated as a senior officer in the Republic. In fact, Franco still loathed the Republic. In his eyes Sanjurjo's biggest crime was not to have staged a coup, but to have botched it. When Sanjurjo asked him to defend him at his subsequent trial, Franco refused and stated *I think that in justice by rebelling and failing you have earned the right to die.*[17] It was an example of Franco's coldness and of how pompous he had become.

Franco's reward for staying out of the plot was a far more prestigious appointment as General Commander (*Comandante general*) of the Balearic Islands. It was a shrewd appointment by Azaña, giving Franco a good job but also keeping him away from the centre of intrigue. Once again Franco was less than grateful, though despite grumbling that he would not take the post he could not resist its status. His main grievance was that a review of past army promotions had just reduced him in the rankings of brigadiers-general from 1st to 24th. Status and prestige was always important to Franco and he took this as another personal affront to his reputation.

While Franco enjoyed the trappings of power in the Balearics, Azaña's centre left administration was forced out of office. Instead, a caretaker centre-right government was formed until new elections were held in November 1933. Franco was tempted to stand as a candidate on a conservative Catholic ticket – though he later tried to deny this – but was persuaded by friends that his best place was in the army. Perhaps he felt his career was going nowhere under the current regime. However, the centre right Radicals did well in the poll and formed the new government under Alejandro Lerroux. Soon the Second Republic would not look quite so bad for Franco.

The following year, 1934, was to prove a momentous one for Franco. On 28 February his mother died from pneumonia while in Madrid. Though he did not display much grief outwardly, Franco was deeply upset at the loss of someone he had loved. Meanwhile his relations with his father were as bad as ever. At the reading of his mother's will Franco had made an effort to be civil with his father, only for the old man to respond with rudeness. It was the last time the two met.

Franco's professional life, however, was far more positive. The new Minister of war Diego Hidalgo was impressed with Franco's professionalism and had him promoted to the rank of major-general. At 41 he was the youngest in Spain. Hidalgo came to rely on his advice and by September Franco was working in Madrid as a special advisor. This meant that he was well placed to play a central role in a crucial episode that both underlined the ever-widening divisions in Spanish society and the way that Franco was prepared to use force against his own countrymen.

During 1934 socialists, communists and the influential anarchists had despaired as even the limited reforms of the previous administration were reversed. The arrival of yet more right-wing members in the government provoked a general strike in early October. The strike, coupled with a short-lived declaration of autonomy in Catalonia, was quickly suppressed except in the mining area of Asturias. The government, which had seemed to expect a revolutionary insurrection, was ready for it. Though technically only an adviser, Franco took effective control of the suppression of the revolt. He quickly deployed troops from both the Legion and the Moroccan *Regulares*. These men, commanded in the field by veteran *Africanista* Colonel Juan Yague, put down the revolutionary movement brutally, as Franco knew they would. Franco was adopting similar tactics to those he had used in Morocco. In particular the brutality of the troops – many of them foreign – during the revolt and subsequent mopping up operations was intended to make the 'enemy' submit. Years later Franco described the campaign in stark terms. It had been a *frontier war against socialism, communism and whatever attacked civilisation in order to replace it with barbarism.*[18]

In all some 4,000 people, including women and children, died in the abortive uprising and tens of thousands were imprisoned. Many were tortured.

For people on the Left, Franco's behaviour marked him out as a hate figure. In contrast the Right hailed Franco as a saviour who had thwarted a communist revolution. If Franco had ever harboured doubts in the past, he held none now. He knew that his mission in life was to save Spain.

Joining the Plot 1935-1936

Franco's merciless suppression of the Asturias revolt cemented his position as the pre-eminent military figure in Spain. It also showed how ruthless he was prepared to be against his own countrymen. His deployment of Moroccan or Moorish troops to fight Spaniards was hugely controversial. One of the great narratives of Spanish history is how, after the Arab/Moorish invasion of the peninsula in the 8th century, Christian Spain had fought back and eventually in 1492 had ended Moorish rule. This process is referred to as the 'Reconquest' (*La Reconquista*). Moreover, the only tiny corner of Spain that was perhaps never conquered by the Moors was a part of Asturias. Thus for Franco – who knew his history well – to use Moroccan troops in that part of the country was doubly symbolic.

The general's total opposition to making concessions to a defeated enemy was also shown after the uprising. Franco was angry when the death sentences handed out to rebellious soldiers were commuted. He said at the time: *The victory is ours and not to apply exemplary punishment to the rebels …would signify trampling on the just rights of the military class and encourage an extremist response.*[19]

Franco had learnt these harsh lessons in Africa and he would use them to devastating effect when he seized control.

For the time being, however, Franco felt there was no need for the military to seize power. He had shown how decisive and brutal action could maintain control. Moreover, while the regime might have been Republican, the politics of the government had shifted to the centre right of the spectrum. For example, one of the key political figures behind the administration in 1934 and 1935 was José Gil Robles, head of the ultra conservative Catholic group CEDA. Reassured by the current turn of events, in late October 1934 Franco used his enhanced prestige on the right to quash plans for another coup, in which Sanjurjo was once again to be the leading figure.

Once more Franco was rewarded for his perceived loyalty to the Republic and in February 1935 was appointed as Commander-in-Chief of the Army of Africa. This meant a welcome return to Morocco for Franco, who saw it as the *most important military command* because of the number of troops and amount of territory involved.[20] It was also a chance to assess at first hand the mood and morale of Spain's premier fighting force.

The African posting did not last long however. When, to the horror of the Left, Gil Robles became Minister of War in May 1935 he immediately used his position to appoint sympathetic senior officers to key jobs. As part of this strategy he appointed Franco to the vital job of Chief of the Central General Staff in Madrid, at the nerve centre of the military. Franco was given the position despite the opposition of the conservatively-inclined President Niceto Alcalá Zamora. In a prophetic turn of phrase, Zamora objected that 'young generals aspire to be fascist caudillos', though he was later to be impressed by Franco's professionalism and loyalty[21]

At the centre of events in Madrid, Franco took great delight in working with Gil Robles to reverse many of his old foe Azaña's reforms of the military. In his words, the young general wanted to *return to the members of the army's units the internal satisfaction that had been lost with the advent of the Republic.*[22] Franco was also keen to learn lessons from the rising in Asturias. He even organised manoeuvres to re-enact the events of 1934. Gil Robles and Franco also ensured that

José Gil Robles (1890 – 1980) was a law professor who in 1933 helped form the alliance of right wing groups known as the Spanish Confederation of Autonomous Rightist Parties (Confederación Española de Derechas Autónimas) or CEDA. This became an extremely influential electoral bloc after the elections of 1933, though Gil Robles never succeeded in becoming prime minister. Gil Robles was a divisive figure whom many on the Left saw as a fascist. CEDA's aim seemed to be to establish a Catholic corporate state. He later became a key adviser to the heir to the Spainish throne Don Juan.

officers sympathetic to the idea of the Republic were removed from key positions, while those opposed to it were promoted. It was at this time too that an old *Africanista* colleague of Franco, General Emilio Mola, who had been discharged from the Army at the start of the Second Republic, was put in charge of the military in Morocco. Mola was to play a key role in the events of 1936.

Many of the measures taken by Franco and Gil Robles were designed not to protect Spain against external threat but to guard against a perceived internal threat. As far as Franco was concerned this threat came from communism. Though he had dismissed the need for a coup in 1934, and while he was confident the army could contain another revolutionary uprising, the ever-calculating Franco decided he needed to keep in close touch with the mood of the army. From the summer of 1935 he was in contact with members of the Spanish Military Union (*Unión Militar Española*) or UME. This was a right-wing organisation of army officers set up to help those who felt threatened by recent reforms. Its importance to Franco was that it had excellent contacts at mid-ranking officer level right through the military as well as with many other right-wing organisations. This gave him the chance to hear about premature coup plots that might play into the hands of the Left. But it also gave him a good idea of just how prepared sympathetic officers were in the event of an uprising. He said that his contacts *allowed one…to know that if one day the life of the nation should be in danger, there were those who would know how to defend it.*[23] That day was not now far away.

In 1935 the fissures in Spanish society had grown far deeper and wider. For example, the tentative attempts at land reforms pursued by the left-leaning first administrations of the Second Republic had barely scratched the surface of the problems of rural poverty. Landless labourers – known as *braceros* – lived in the most abject of conditions in areas such as Extremadura and Andalusia. Some preferred to inhabit pigsties because they were better than their own homes. Even if they found work they might labour a full day in the blazing sun for just three pesetas. Others toiled for still less, perhaps only one peseta a day, or even just soup and a lump of bread. In fact, according to one newspaper at the time, some peasants had to eat grass to stay alive.[24] Meanwhile much of Spain's land was owned by a small group of massive landowners, who often left huge swathes of it untilled.

By November 1935 the centre and left had decided to try to set aside their differences and work to remove such injustices, which were mirrored across many parts of society. Aware that a lack of unity had let them down in the past they joined forces in an electoral pact known as the Popular Front.

As the Left recovered the unity of earlier years, the right-leaning administration meanwhile was beginning to fall apart. Prime Minister Lerroux and his radicals had long been tainted with corruption and in September 1935 the President Alcalá Zamora dismissed him.

Gil Robles hoped that the time had finally come for him to head the government but the President – who never trusted the CEDA leader - ultimately opted to call national elections for 16 February 1936. Gil Robles was so enraged at seeing power slip from his grasp that he actively considered the possibility of a coup. Significantly, one of the key voices who dissuaded him was General Franco. This was not because the Chief of General Staff felt a coup would be morally wrong, but because he could not be sure that it would yet have enough support in the army. However, Franco was genuinely sad to see Gil Robles step down as Minister of War and in a farewell speech even shed a sentimental tear as he claimed that the army *had never felt itself better led in this period.*[25]

After the Asturias rising the Republican Manuel Azaña was briefly imprisoned by the government, making him a political martyr of the Left. The enthusiastic reception to a series of rousing speeches by Azaña in 1935 convinced the Left that they could achieve unity. Therefore left of centre Republicans, Socialists and Communists agreed on an electoral pact known as the Popular Front. It was approved of but not created by the Soviet-backed Communist International (Comintern). The Front won a huge majority in the Spanish parliament (Cortes) in the February 1936 elections, even though it had only a narrow majority of the popular vote.

The February elections were held in a highly charged atmosphere. The

Right had quickly made up its mind that the Popular Front was nothing less than a front for a communist revolution, despite its disparate membership. For its part the Left feared a military coup and or fascist dictatorship. Under the intense gravitational pull of the Left and Right, the centre of Spanish politics had all but crumbled.

During the campaign Franco felt that a military uprising was almost, if not quite, inevitable, though his natural caution held him back from committing to any timetable. Late in January he visited London to represent the Spanish Government at the funeral of George V. On the way back he spoke of his fears to the Spanish Military Attaché in Paris Major Antonio Barroso. He repeated the prevailing though incorrect view on the right that the Popular Front was a direct creation of Comintern and that if the *worst came to the worst it would be the duty [of the army] to intervene.* He told his eager listener: *If you hear of me going to Africa you'll know that we have decided there's no other way but a rising.*[26] Such remarks suggest that, at the very least, Franco had discussed with other senior officers the broad outlines of how a coup might take place.

On 17 February news of the Popular Front's victory brought thousands of supporters onto the streets in celebration. Though these were simply spontaneous expressions of joy, many on the Right feared that it was a sign that the much-feared revolution was on its way. Certainly this was what Franco seems to have felt. In the hours immediately afterwards the Chief of General Staff tried hard to get the outgoing administration to allow the military to intervene. He even – quite illegally – managed to get martial law declared briefly in parts of Spain despite the fact it had not been authorised by interim Prime Minister Manuel Portela's government. It was an unusually incautious action for the prudent Franco, and a sign of how serious he felt the situation was. Quickly, however, and once it was clear his gambit had failed, he reverted to his usual caution. He blithely assured the prime minister's office that he was not interested in politics but simply with military affairs.[27]

However, at this time in the country's history neither Franco nor the rest of Spain could escape politics. The new prime minister was Franco's old enemy

Manuel Azaña, but the radical politician had little time for triumphalism. The unity that had impelled the Left to their impressive electoral victory evaporated almost over night when the Socialists refused to take part in the Government. Partly this was due to rivalry between the two leading socialists Indalecio Prieto and the more radical Francisco Largo Caballero. Largo Caballero was naively confident that the main socialist party the Spanish Workers' Socialist Party (*Partido Socialista Obrero Español* – PSOE) would soon be able to form a government of its own. The result was that not only did Azaña's administration attract the inevitable deep suspicion of the Right, it only had limited support from the Left.

The astute Azaña realised that the threat of a military coup was greater than ever and one of his first steps was to move potentially dangerous senior officers as far away as possible from the centre of power. One of these officers was Franco. To his disgust if not his surprise Franco lost his position as Chief of the Central General Staff and was instead made General Commander of the Canary Islands.

Though in theory it was not a bad posting for a relatively new major-general, Franco saw his removal to the far-flung group of islands off the African coast as yet another slight from his old enemy. He was later to complain that he felt like a *prisoner in the Canaries*.[28] Before he left, the general was obliged to pay a courtesy visit to both the President Alcala Zamora and to Azaña. Both meetings were tense affairs. Franco later accused the Prime Minister of having been dangerously complacent about the threats that faced Spain. Meanwhile, in his interview with the President, Franco claims to have told him: *Of one thing I am certain, and I can guarantee, that whatever circumstances may arise, wherever I am, there will be no Communism.*[29] Such a pronouncement underlined Franco's sense of self-importance and growing certainty that he alone could guarantee Spain's future safety.

One of Franco's last acts before leaving for his new job was to meet fellow senior generals, including Mola, at the Madrid home of a prominent CEDA supporter. The officers discussed the chances of a coup, and yet again the absent Sanjurjo – who was still in exile – was chosen as its figurehead.

Portrait of Franco. 1936

Franco's input appears to have been minimal other than suggesting that the uprising should not cloak itself in any particular political labels. Indeed the ever-cautious Franco had not even committed himself to joining it at this stage. Instead General Mola emerged as the prime mover of the plot.

Franco's caution – which bordered on chronic indecision – would continue right up to the last minute. It soon became a subject of bitter amusement among the senior officers who were committed to a coup and they dubbed him 'Miss Canary Islands 1936' for his apparent coyness over joining them.[30] Much of this reluctance stemmed from Franco's realistic concern that any such uprising would be a long and bloody affair, given the opposition they would face. This was brought home to the general even as he arrived in Cadiz in March 1936 to take a boat to the Canaries. Anarchists had attacked churches and torched a convent and Franco angrily criticised the local military commander for having let this happen. Though the officer protested that he had been under order from civilian authorities not to get involved, Franco refused to shake his hand. Franco then had a taste of own status with the Left when he, Carmen, Nenuca and the faithful Pacón disembarked at Tenerife. They were greeted by protestors whose banners proclaimed him the 'butcher of Asturias', after the events of October 1934.

Yet despite the feverish political atmosphere and the incessant talk of likely coups. Franco and his entourage settled down to an oddly ordinary lifestyle. Though Franco worked hard in his day job, improving the island's defences in case of a European war, he and Carmen enjoyed a hectic social life amid the pleasant spring climate of the islands. And it was while in the Canary Islands that Franco developed a passion for playing golf that was to last for the rest of his life. He took regular lessons and as late as early July he was planning a trip to the home of golf, Scotland, to improve his game. The general also began English lessons three times a week with a local teacher, and combined his two new interests by learning English golfing vocabulary. Such everyday behaviour sat oddly with the image of a man who was about to try to overthrow the state.

For a while, in fact, Franco's mind was more on civilian politics than on armed rebellion. In the early 1930s he had flirted with the idea of standing for election, and in April 1936 the re-run of an election in Cuenca persuaded him to stand as a CEDA candidate. He only withdrew after objections from José Antonio Primo de Rivera, leader of the small but growing Spanish fascist party called the Falange (the Spanish word for phalanx). José Antonio, the charismatic son of the former dictator, was in jail and wanted to win the re-run election to gain the immunity from prosecution granted to members of the Cortes. Though Franco agreed to stand aside, he never forgot or forgave José Antonio, whom he had already met and instantly disliked. The episode also proved embarrassing in later years for Franco when he justified much of his regime's structure on the basis of the weakness of democracy. He therefore made several efforts to re-write history, bizarrely claiming at one point he had considered standing as a deputy simply so he could have *more direct contact* with army garrisons at the start of the uprising.[31]

Politicians on the Left such as Prieto saw Franco as the soldier most likely to spearhead an uprising against the Second Republic. In a speech the socialist declared that the general was 'young and gifted' and had a 'network of friends in the Army'. Prieto concluded that 'at a given moment [he] has it in him to lead such a movement with maximum probable success because of the prestige he enjoys'.[32] Coming from a political enemy rather than one of Franco's sycophantic supporters, these comments are a good indication of how Franco was regarded in Spain in early 1936 – even if it was not a view shared by all his senior army colleagues. They were still struggling to get him to commit to the very uprising that Prieto feared.

As the summer approached, General Mola contained his plans for a coup while in Madrid Azaña became President. A parallel move to make Prieto Prime Minister had foundered on the rock of Largo Caballero's opposition, squandering a chance to bring some breadth to the Government's support and some coherence to its policies. From now on the administration would be increasingly irrelevant to the events that unfolded.

For his part Franco fretted about the state of Spain – the growing unrest in both cities and the countryside – but worried too about what could be done about it. In June he sent an extraordinary letter to the new Prime Minister Santiago Casares Quiroga, whose fragile health seemed to sum up the state of the country's democracy. The convoluted letter raised a number of specific concerns about the way the military was being treated at the time, and warned darkly about the Army's *professional disquiet*. But it also appeared to suggest that if Franco was put in charge of the military then the safety of the Fatherland could be ensured, removing the likelihood of any plots. The purpose of the letter is open to interpretation, full as it is of Franco's usual ambiguity. But one view is that it was intended to give him some political cover in the event of any coup failing; he would be able to claim that he had tried to warn the Government in advance. That would have been very typical of Franco's cautious strategy.[33]

By the time of the June letter – to which the Prime Minister never replied – Mola's plans were well advanced. Various generals had been allocated their areas to seize while Sanjurjo was earmarked to be the new Head of State. By early July Mola and other conspirators had even begun the arrangements to fly Franco away from the Canaries. The London correspondent of the Spanish newspaper *ABC* Luis Bolín chartered a Dragon Rapide aircraft in Croydon on 6 July. To provide convincing cover for the flight a retired British army officer Hugh Pollard plus his daughter Diana and a friend flew on board posing as holidaymakers. By 12 July the plane had reached Casablanca in Morocco, en route for the Canaries.

There was however one small snag in Mola's plan; General Franco had still not agreed to join the coup. As a prominent figure in the army with unrivalled prestige in the crucial Army of Africa, Franco was considered an important, possibly essential member of the coup. But as late as 12 July, the day that 'Franco's plane' landed in Africa, the general indicated to Mola he would not join.

Within 48 hours, however, Franco had became a full and enthusiastic member of the plot. What changed his mind was political violence in Madrid. On 12 July Falangist gunmen had shot and murdered a member of the Second Republic's new Assault Guards. Early the next day members of the Assault Guard took revenge by kidnapping and killing prominent right-wing politician José Calvo Sotelo. Though it was in no way sanctioned by the authorities, the brutal killing sparked outrage on the Right. The date of the coup had long been fixed for 18 July but the murder of Calvo Sotelo was a perfect 'excuse' for it. It also shocked Franco and galvanized him into action. His English teacher Dora Lennard recalled how after the

Franco's favourite Moorish guard enter Salamanca in style

shooting she found him a 'changed man'. She said: 'He looked ten years older...for the first time he came near to losing his iron self-control and unalterable serenity.'[34]

Franco quickly told his fellow senior officers, including Mola who was in Pamplona, that he was now with them. Nearly all the pieces were now in place. However, Franco faced a serious practical problem. The general was based in Santa Cruz, the capital of Tenerife. However, to avoid suspicion and keep clear of Tenerife's fog, on 14 July 'holidaymaker' Hugh Pollard's Dragon Rapide had landed instead on the island of Gran Canaria to the east. The problem was that to travel from one island to the next Franco needed the permission of the Ministry of War. As Franco had just carried out an inspection tour on Gran Canaria he would not get permission to make a second trip so soon. Franco was thus stranded on Tenerife while the plane waiting to take him to save Spain was waiting on another island. To reach Gran Canaria and the Dragon Rapide Franco would need either a stroke of luck or foul play.

Taking Control 1936-1937

The military coup of July 1936 could have taken a very different course if Franco had been left stranded on Tenerife. Indeed had the general been unable to lead the Army of Africa at all it is possible that the revolt would have failed. The history of Spain would then have been very different. That Franco was able to leave Tenerife was thanks to the extraordinarily coincidental death of the military commander on Gran Canaria, where his plane was waiting for him. General Amado Balmes, reputedly an expert shot, was killed in an incident at a shooting range. This meant Franco, his family and loyal senior officers had the perfect excuse to travel to Las Palmas on Gran Canaria to attend the unfortunate general's funeral without attracting suspicion.

Balmes' death has never been adequately explained. It is possible that it was, as claimed, simply an accident and that Balmes shot himself while trying to free a jammed pistol, though given his experience this seems slightly implausible. It is also feasible that Balmes was murdered to provide a pretext for Franco to link up with his plane. Franco had shown in Africa and would show many times in the future that he had no qualms about the cold-blooded killing of people if their death suited his aims.

The truth about Balmes's death will probably never be known. The outcome was clear, however. On 17 July Franco, his family and entourage were on Gran Canaria ready for the start of the uprising. The coup was in fact timed for the next day, but rebel officers in Africa started their uprising on the evening of the 17th after they feared the plot had been uncovered. Franco was awoken with the news and he immediately dashed off a telegram to garrisons all over Spain. It read simply: *Glory to the Army of Africa. Spain above all. Receive the enthusiastic greeting of these garrisons which join with you and the rest of our companions in the Peninsula in these historic moments.*

Blind faith in victory. Long live Spain with honour. General Franco.[35]

The rebels were keen to broadcast the fact that a prestigious general such as Franco – and the Army of Africa – had joined them to help bring any wavering officers on side. After his many doubts Franco was acting decisively, like a man who has awoken from a slumber. Yet even now the general's caution was apparent. Nowhere in the telegram nor in a subsequent hasty manifesto was there direct mention of overthrowing the democratically constituted Republic. Instead there was a reference to stamping out anarchy, an arguably legitimate role for the military. Even at this late stage Franco was trying to keep his options open should the coup fail.

With Carmen and nine-year-old Nenuca safely on board a naval vessel, and ultimately bound for Le Havre, Franco still had to get from Las Palmas to the airfield where the Dragon Rapide awaited. This was far from straightforward. News of the uprising had reached and enraged Republican supporters who started to converge on the town where fighting ensued. It was impossible to travel by road to the aircraft because the villages on the way were strongholds of Republican support. Instead Franco and his entourage had to make their way by sea in a small tug boat. Eventually they arrived at the small airport where ex-RAF pilot Captain William Henry Bebb was awaiting to take Franco and the loyal Pacón to Africa. It took off just after 2pm.

On board the aircraft Franco and Pacón took off their army uniforms and donned suits, with the general posing as a diplomat in case the plane was intercepted. As part of the 'disguise', Franco put on a pair of glasses and also shaved off his trademark moustache. This later prompted the sardonic comment from General Gonzalo Queipo de Llano that his moustache was the only thing that Franco ever sacrificed for his country. Having stopped at Agadir and then Casablanca, the Dragon Rapide eventually arrived over Tetuán early on the morning of Sunday 19 July. Even now Franco was not out of danger as he and the crew of the circling aircraft were not sure who held control of the airport, the rebels or the Republicans. Eventually Franco spied the familiar mop of hair of an old *Africanista* officer he knew and trusted and declared: *We can land – I've just seen blondy!*[36]

Rapturously greeted by his old soldiers from the Army of Africa, there was now no going back for Franco. Franco and other senior officers were intent on overthrowing the legitimate government and regime of Spain, the very course of action he had warned his brother Ramón against just a few years earlier. Franco's main justification for doing this was his conviction that Spain was about to be taken over by communists. Ironically, but quite predictably, it was only after the coup started that parts of Spain came under the effective control of communists and anarchists as they took up arms against the rebels' illegal uprising.

Just as the elections of recent years had split Spain in two, so the military uprising caused a major rift. The Army itself was torn, with many senior officers staying loyal to the Republic; indeed Franco was one of only four major generals out of a total of 21 to join the rebellion. Large parts of the Navy also stayed loyal to the Republic, as did many in the Civil Guard.

Emilio Mola Vidal (1887–1937) was a career soldier, a veteran of Africa and a close contemporary of Franco's. The two men respected each other's abilities as soldiers and they shared similar views about the problems of Spain. Mola became the main organiser of the 1936 coup but his doubts about its likely success and his poor initial handling of German and Italian allies handed Franco the initiative. A few years after his death in a plane crash Hitler remarked that out of the two Spanish generals it had been Mola who was the 'real brains, the real leader'. [37]

The country was split geographically, with the rebels finding success in conservative areas such as the Navarre where Mola was based and in towns such as Salamanca, Segovia and Burgos, plus in Franco's native Galicia. Yet much of Spain, including large cities such as Madrid, Barcelona and Valencia, the Asturias, the Basque country and much of the south stayed loyal to the Republic. After a few days, the rebels controlled little more than a third of Spain. Though the government and its representatives dithered extraordinarily, many workers groups and Left wing organisations took the initiative and took to the streets to defend the Republic.

Just as the success of the uprising was not guaranteed, Franco's leadership of it was by no means inevitable either. The figurehead was General Sanjurjo, who incidentally viewed Franco as untrustworthy and self-interested, while the plot's prime mover was General Mola.

There were also other senior generals involved, notably General Miguel Cabanellas, who led the rising in Zaragoza, and the independently-minded Queipo Llano who seized control in Seville. In fact Franco himself had told Sanjurjo in the early summer that the height of his ambition was to become the new High Commissioner in Morocco once the coup was successful. Thus nobody, perhaps not even Franco, imagined on 18 July that the diminutive general from Galicia would soon become the dominant figure in the rebellion.

It was a mixture of chance events and Franco's own dynamic seizure of the initiative that soon changed the landscape. First, the portly Sanjurjo was killed on 20 July when the tiny bi-plane in which he was to fly to Spain from Portugal crashed on take-off and burst into flames. The loss of the undisputed figurehead dramatically opened up the field for others.

Then there was the patchy success of the rebellion itself, which was already assuming the mantle of a civil war rather than a coup. Mola should have had a decisive advantage over Franco from the start. At least his army was on the Peninsula while Franco's much-trumpeted Army of Africa was stranded on the wrong side of the straits of Gibraltar where the mostly Republican navy barred the way. Yet from the first moment he landed in Africa Franco had exuded an air of supreme confidence in the certainty of rebel victory. Franco's sedentary lifestyle may have led to him developing a pot belly and double chin, and his squeaky voice and stature were as unimpressive as ever. Yet the old decisive fighter from Africa days was back, and his confidence was infectious among his officers and men. Within minutes of landing at Tetuán, Franco had scribbled a shopping list of planes and bombs that he authorised Luis Bolin to try to buy in Rome, Berlin or even London if necessary. After Sanjurjo's death, Franco's confident manner persuaded both Mussolini and Hitler that he was the sole person to deal with on the rebels' side.

Franco was no less bold when it came to getting his stranded Army across to mainland Spain. Using a mixture of German and Italian aircrafts from his new friends, Franco staged the first major airlift in history of its kind and flew men and materials to the mainland. From July until October more than 800 flights – many involving German Junkers Ju-52 aircraft – took some 14,000 men across the Straits. On 5 August Franco also gambled that the Republican fleet, manned by inexperienced sailors who had rebelled against their pro-rebel officers, would be unwilling to risk being attacked by aircraft. He was right, and from that date regular convoys brought yet more men to the Peninsula.

The Army of Africa, under the command of the ruthless Colonel Juan Yagüe and with its contingent of Moroccan mercenaries, was now unleashed. It soon made rapid and bloody progress northwards up through Andalusia and then Extremadura. The troops used the same tactics that Franco had employed in Africa and also in Asturias in 1934 – utter ruthlessness and terror. While Franco set up his headquarters in a palatial house at a safe distance in Seville, the legionnaires and mercenaries butchered and murdered their way through small towns, villages and countryside. In Badajoz, one of the bloodiest scenes of the early conflict, 1,500 supposed enemy militants were rounded up in the bullring and shot in cold blood. Meanwhile the bodies of the dead were searched for valuables, and soldiers used rifle butts to smash out the gold teeth of corpses. These atrocities grimly brought to life Franco's words to an American journalist on 27 July in which the general had spoken of his intention to *save Spain from Marxism at whatever cost*. When the reporter suggested this might entail shooting half of the country, Franco coolly replied: *I repeat, at whatever cost*.[38] For Franco this was an extension of the colonial war he had fought in Africa, only this time the enemy was any of his fellow countrymen who happened to disagree with his view of how to govern Spain.

Wrapped up in the demands of the war, Franco soon had little time for other matters. He worked long hours, acquiring a curious reputation he would keep for decades of being able to work for hours at a desk without needing to go to relieve himself. Nor were calls of nature the only thing that had to take second place to Franco's priorities. When after a two-month exile Carmen and Nenuca finally returned to Spain to see him, Franco kept them waiting for an hour because he had important visitors.

The strategy of the rebels, who came to style themselves Nationalists, was for Franco's Army of the South to link up with Mola's Army of the North and then to move eastwards and attack Madrid. At this time the Republican side was in political disarray. When the Prime Minister Casares Quiroga was informed of the uprising in July he allegedly went off to lie down. He resigned on 19 July and two more premiers followed in quick order before the man dubbed the 'Spanish Lenin' Largo Caballero became Prime Minister on 4 September. Till then the Republicans had lacked a coherent centralised response to the rebellion.

Yet while Franco wanted the Nationalists to take Madrid, there were other thoughts on his mind too. The death of Sanjurjo and Franco's growing status with Germany and Italy had convinced the already self-important general that he was the man to lead the rebellion to 'save' Spain. Since his days as an African military hero in the press, Franco had been very aware of the importance of image and public perception. Staff at his closely-controlled headquarters encouraged the foreign press to talk about Franco as the 'commander in chief' of the Nationalists. This was despite the fact he was technically just one member of the Defence Committee set up to co-ordinate strategy. His officers and advisers, who included his own brother Nicolás, Yague, Millán Astray and the creator of the Spanish Air Force General Alfredo Kindelán actively promoted Franco's cause. When Franco flew to visit Mola in Burgos on 16 August both men would have been very aware of the rapturous reception that Franco received from the local population. Franco was probably relieved early in September when Mola's forces were checked on their march on Madrid after stiffer Republican resistance. It would have been unbearable had his main rival won such a prize. Instead Franco sought a propaganda coup of his own. He soon spotted an opportunity in Toledo.

Since the start of the revolt loyal Republicans had forced around 1,000 Civil Guards and Falange militia to retreat into the fortress – or Alcázar – in Toledo. As each day passed the plight of these Nationalists seemed more

Franco with Generals Moschardo and Varela after the relief of Toledo

desperate. In military terms Toledo was unimportant and the Nationalist army could easily have passed it by as they sped from Extremadura via the town of Talavera towards Madrid; the Army of Africa had already advanced more than 300 miles in four weeks. Yet it was here that Franco had started his army career, and more importantly Toledo was the centre of Spanish Catholicism. Thus the wily Franco could see a chance for a great public relations exercise. Accordingly on 21 September he ordered his troops to divert east to lift the siege of Toledo.

Franco's decision to delay the attack on a virtually defenceless Madrid

The Nationalists, including a handful of cadets, were trapped inside the massively thick walls of the old fortress while Republicans wasted time, ammunition and lives trying to capture it. War correspondents were barred from watching the Nationalist's relieving attack, led by General Enrique Varela on 27 September, and which was merciless. No prisoners were taken, Republicans were beheaded and the streets literally ran with blood. Around 200 wounded Republicans were killed with hand grenades as they lay in hospital. One of the besieged Colonel Moscardo famously greeted General Varela with the words: 'Nothing to report at the Alcázar' ('Sin novedad en el Alcázar').[39]

Franco and his Moorish cavalcade pass through Salamanca. 1937

while he relieved the Alcázar can only be understood in terms of his emerging personal strategy. Now that the coup had turned into a civil war, it was less important for the war to be won quickly than for it to be won on Franco's terms. He wanted every inch of Spain taken from the Republicans and 'cleansed' – a hangover from Africa days – while he consolidated his position at the top of the revolt. Relieving the besieged Nationalists was an international propaganda coup that gave Franco a great opportunity to do both. Later that year Franco conceded that the relief of Toledo was a *military error* but one that had been made *deliberately*.[40]

On the day that Franco ordered the diversion to Toledo, he had met other members of the Defence Committee in a wooden cabin at an airfield near Salamanca to discuss the overall command of the war. Significantly, Franco and his 'campaign team' had called for the meeting. Eventually the committee agreed that the efficient conduct of the war demanded a single commander-in-chief or 'Generalísimo' rather than a committee. The question was, who?

The senior general and nominal chairman of the committee General Miguel Cabanellas was discounted because he had supported the Republic and was suspected of being a freemason. In any case he saw no need for a sole commander. Queipo de Llano had also supported the Republic while Mola's conduct of the war had not been impressive and he had angered the sizeable monarchist contingent by banishing Alfonso XIII's heir Don Juan from Spain. The only candidate who was convincingly conservative, Catholic, monarchist and had a near-exemplary war record was Franco. Thus with the exception of the abstaining Cabanellas, all the other generals voted for Franco to be Generalísimo.

However, there were important caveats to Franco's new position. It was clearly understood that the position was a temporary one until the end of the war. Also, the decision was not broadcast, which naturally reduced the effectiveness of the new post. There was a clear reluctance to grant anyone full powers lest they become, as Cabanellas for one feared, a dictator.

This interim decision deeply disappointed Franco's 'campaign team' who wanted their man to be both military chief and head of state. Kindalán, Millán Astray, Nicolás Franco and Yagüe succeeded in getting a second meeting of the committee fixed for 28 September. Yet Franco himself was worried. Though there is little doubt that he desperately wanted to be named head of state – an opportunity that would have seemed fanciful a little more than two months ago – now he hesitated. Once again Franco's innate caution was the reason. The

Franco takes the oath as he is proclaimed head of the Nationalist government. 1936

general was terrified of overplaying his hand and risking his current position as Generalísimo. The usually loyal but always outspoken Yague now threatened to pledge the Foreign Legion's vital support to

another candidate if Franco did not pursue power more vigorously.

In the end, a combination of events and the campaign team's careful planning won the day. On the evening of 27 September Franco was able to salute ecstatic crowds at his new palatial HQ in Cáceres as the acclaimed hero of the Alcázar, even though he had been nowhere near the fighting. The next day his team had organised an impressive guard of honour at the Salamanca airfield for the hero of the hour. Kindalán then presented the other generals with a proposal that Franco became Chief of State. Eventually, after much persuasion, the other officers agreed to sign a document granting Franco full powers as Head of the Government of the Spanish State. The original proposal was that Franco would be given these powers while the war lasted, though when the decree was later published those words were absent, possibly deleted by Franco himself. In any case from now on Franco ignored the niceties of his title and acted as Head of State. It was, Franco declared, the *most important moment of my life.*[41]

None of the other generals shared Franco's excitement, a gloomy Mola included. But it was Franco's old commanding officer Cabanellas who was most adamant about the error they had committed. 'You don't know what you've just done because you don't know him like I do...If as you wish you give him Spain, he is going to believe that it is his and he won't let anyone replace him either during the war or after until he is dead.'[42] Indeed, Franco now had almost absolute power in Spain – or at least those parts of Spain that the Nationalists had so far managed to conquer.

On 1 October Generalísimo was formally invested as Chief of State in a ceremony full of pomp and at which he promised *no home without a light or a Spaniard without bread.* However, in a later radio broadcast he hinted strongly at what was to come politically, namely a totalitarian regime.[43] The trappings of this came soon enough. Franco adopted the title '*Caudillo*' – warrior leader – clearly aping the titles of his allies, Hitler the Fuehrer in German and Mussolini the Duce in Italy. Pictures of the new leader were put up all over Nationalist regions as the cult of his personality was developed. At his newest HQ, the magnificent bishop's palace in Salamanca, Franco's own loyal Moorish Guard of Moroccan troops stood guard.

Yet while Franco revelled in his new powers he faced a difficult winter. Already Hitler and Mussolini were privately irritated at the Nationalists' inability to finish off the Republic. Franco's decision to seize Toledo, though important for his own aims, had delayed the attack on Madrid for

Nationalist troops suppress resistance to their advance in the streets of Lerida

at least two weeks. This was to prove very costly.

On 7 October the Nationalist forces, under the overall command of Mola, finally started the advance on the capital. Despite the delays foreign observers fully expected that Madrid would fall quickly. Even when the talented Republican Lieutenant-Colonel Vicente Rojo – a former colleague of Franco's – began to marshal the city's defences, and Soviet tanks and foreign volunteers stiffened the defenders' resolve, few expected Madrid

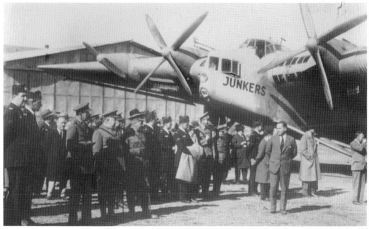

Nationalist Generals inspecting German plane

to hold out. The Republicans were bombarded and demoralised by the bombing of German planes and on 6 November Largo Caballero and his government fled for Valencia. Members of the international press corps were so convinced that Madrid was on the verge of falling that some filed reports that it already had. One Portuguese radio broadcast eloquently 'described' Franco's triumphant entry of the city on his trademark white horse.

However, aided by the chance discovery by Republicans of the Nationalist battle plan in a captured tank, the attack was repulsed. The seemingly invincible Army of Africa was halted in the west of the city and many of its soldiers died in brutal fighting. As he surveyed the carnage the badly injured Nationalist officer Major Antonio Castejón despairingly told American journalist John Whitaker: 'We made this revolt, and now we are beaten'.[44]

By 22 November it was clear that the massive attack against Madrid had failed and a sense of gloom fell upon the Nationalist cause. General Franco may have become Spain's *de facto* Head of State, but to govern the whole of the country he had first to win the war. At the start of 1937 that prospect still looked a long way off.

Total Victory 1937-39

As his military campaign faltered at the start of 1937, Franco was fortunate that the complex political situation in Europe favoured his cause. It is true that Soviet tanks, other war materials and advisers undoubtedly helped sustain the Republican side, even if they paid dearly for it by sending much of Spain's gold reserves to Russia for 'safe-keeping'. Yet it was the intervention, or rather non-intervention, of France and Britain that was crucial. The British did not want to provoke Italy and particularly Germany into a larger conflict by getting involved in Spain. France, who had shown initial sympathy with the Republican plight and sent some arms, fell in line with the policy set by London. Thus from as early as August 1936 there was an agreed policy of non-intervention. The fact that Germany and Italy brazenly broke the agreement was generally overlooked, and their military support hugely outweighed the Soviet aid. Stalin's backing enabled the Republicans to survive – for a while – but was never enough for them to win. In contrast much of international public opinion sided with the Republicans who argued that this conflict was about defeating the rise of fascism which was already on the march throughout Europe. This led to the formation of the International Brigades.

Despite their vital support, Franco nonetheless had a complex relationship with his German and Italian backers. He admired German military prowess and was often adulatory about Mussolini. But the proud Spaniard was deeply irritated when Italian soldiers and black-shirted fascist militia operated almost as a separate army. For their part Hitler and Mussolini often found the attitude of their unpredictable and occasionally ungrateful Spanish ally hard to fathom. On one occasion, when learning that six thousand Black Shirts were being sent, Franco said sulkily to an Italian officer: *Who requested them? When one sends troops to a friendly country one at least asks permission.*[45] Franco was especially galled when crowing Italian troops gained an easy victory at Málaga in early February 1937. His propagandists sought to attribute Nationalist successes to the discovery of a holy relic – the hand of 16th century Spanish saint St Teresa of Avila – in the city. The superstitious Franco had it sent to him and kept it close by him for the rest of his life. Much as he needed foreign aid, Franco was always determined that the Nationalist victory should be seen as a Spanish and more particularly a Franco triumph.

More costly military setbacks around Madrid in the late winter and early spring of 1937 at Jarama and Guadalajara – in which Franco's unaccountable failure to support them contributed to a bad defeat for Italian troops – convinced Franco that he needed to settle in for a long war of attrition. As he told the perplexed Italians he wanted to cleanse the country not just to win quick victories.[46] First however he needed to cement his position at the centre of the new Spain he was fighting to create. Franco did not want any civilian rivals getting in the way once the fighting was over, and he also needed to bring some political cohesion to the Nationalist cause. For while it was clear that the July coup was a right-wing blow *against* communism and anarchy, it was less easy to say what the revolt was *for*.

A total of 35,000 foreigners fought for the Republican cause during the Spanish Civil War, the volunteers coming from 53 different countries. The most numerous were the French, who provided some 10,000 members of the Brigades, while there were around 5,000 Poles, a similar number of Germans and Austrian, 3,000 Americans and 2,000 British. The main motivation for most of the volunteers was to take part in a fight against the spread of fascism. The survivors left Spain in November 1938. Prominent people who took part included the British writer George Orwell who later wrote Homage to Catalonia about his experiences.

Divisions among the senior officers reflected the contrasting views of the Spanish Right. There were monarchists who supported the return of Alfonso or his heir Don Juan, and others who supported the Carlist cause. (The Carlists were the followers of the 19th century pretender Don Carlos and his successors and who favoured an absolutist state; their militia played a prominent and bloody role in the uprising.) Their organisation was

Ernest Hemingway stands with his back to the camera amongst a group of the International Brigade

known as the Traditionalist Communion (Communión Traditionalista). Another grouping were members of groups such as CEDA, who favoured a Catholic corporatist state.

Then there were the Falangists. The Falange, Spain's fascist party, had been a relatively small organisation up to 1936 and its charismatic leader José Antonio Primo de Rivera was shot by the Republicans in November 1936. The role of its trigger-happy militias, however, had enormously increased its power in the civil war. They were naturally opposed to the restoration of the monarchy and favoured a radical one-party system similar to that of Germany or Italy.

One might have assumed that Franco's sympathies would be all on the side of the monarchists or of the Catholics. He was religious, a loyal supporter of the king, deeply conservative and had hitherto shown little interest in the ideology of fascism. However, the Falange held some attractions for him. It was ardently anti-communist and was a popular-based organisation that Franco could use to wield influence. As a result of his alliance the Caudillo was also becoming interested in the political systems adopted by Germany and Italy. The Falangists' anti-monarchism was also not necessarily a problem for Franco. Despite his past views, he was increasingly disinclined to share power with anyone, and that included a king.

Franco was to use the different aims of the Right to maintain his grip on power. He skilfully held out the prospect of the return of a king to keep the monarchists happy while at the same time promising enough to keep the Falangists on board. His first step along this political tight rope act was in December 1936 when he brought the various factions' militias under military control. His second in the spring of 1937 was to create one party or 'Movement' that combined the different rightist traditions. On 18 April 1937 he announced its formation under the cumbersome name of the Spanish Traditionalist Phalanx of Committees for National Syndicalist Attack (Falange Española Tradicionalista y de las Juntas de Ofensiva Nacional-Sindicalista – FET y de las JONS). Franco himself was its leader. This new movement merged the Falangists and the Carlist Traditionalist Communion, and dissolved other right-wing organisations such as CEDA whose members automatically became members of the new body.

In achieving this Franco showed just how brilliant a politician he could be. He completely out-manoeuvred the ambitious but naïve key figure in the Falange Manuel Hedilla, who until the last minute believed that he would be head of a single fascist party that would dominate the new Spain. Instead the thuggish Hedilla was arrested and only narrowly avoided being shot when a reluctant Franco was persuaded that his execution would simply make Hedilla a martyr among his working class supporters. The episode showed how well Franco had absorbed the lessons of Africa where manipulating the shifting allegiances of various groups and tribes was an essential part of military survival. The legal formation of the new movement was also the occasion on which Franco's elegant brother-in-law Ramón Serrano Suñer first made his mark.

With his political hold more or less secure, Franco once more turned his attentions back to the war. His aim was to take the country a bit at a time, or *town by town, village by village, railway by railway* as he put it.[48] In many ways this was a re-run of the medieval *Reconquista*, the gradual retaking of land from the enemy. The first target was the north and the Basque country in particular where much of the country's heavy industry was located. Republican sympathisers put up strong resistance and initially the Nationalists' progress was slow. But they were supported by Germany's crack Condor Legion who were keen to show just how effective their new tactic of terror bombing could be. As the Basque defenders eventually retreated under sustained bombing and artillery attack they became bunched up around a small but historic market town. It was here that the most infamous incident of the Spanish Civil War took place – the bombing of Guernica.

Franco, who was safe inside the comfort of his Salamanca palace,

Ramón Serrano Suñer 1901–2003 became Franco's brother-in-law when he married Carmen Polo's attractive younger sister Zita. The slightly-built but handsome Serrano was an accomplished lawyer who was arrested by the Republicans in Madrid. He managed to escape and in February 1937 began work making some constitutional sense of Franco's new regime. In doing so he replaced Franco's bon vivant brother Nicolás. Franco grew increasingly mistrustful of the intelligent Serrano, and was doubtless dismayed by Carmen's habit of saying in family discussions: 'Shut up Paco (Franco's nickname) and listen to what Ramón is saying'.[47]

reacted to the international outrage over the bombing of Guernica by first denying that it had even happened. When this proved untenable, the Nationalists then claimed that the Republicans had blown up the town themselves. From then on Franco would always deny that he had authorised the German Condor Legion to carry out the attack, even though all the evidence suggests the general knew perfectly well what the German tactics were. As Commander-in-Chief Franco was ultimately responsible for the destruction of Guernica.

Though the incessant bombing affected Basque morale, its people kept fighting and it was not until 19 June that Nationalist troops were able to enter Bilbao and to take control of the region's valuable industry and mineral wealth. Even now the Basque army refused to surrender and continued fighting as it retreated westwards towards Santender. It was here that Franco once again demonstrated his obsessive refusal to show any magnaminity towards his own defeated countrymen.

Guernica was the spiritual capital of the Basque people, where an assembly used to meet under the town's ancient oak tree. The sustained bombing by German and Italian aircraft on the afternoon of 26 April took place as local peasants were attending market. The attack was intended to deal a devastating blow to the morale of the Basque people. In all some 1,685 people were killed and 900 injured in the raid. The bombing caused an outcry because of the presence of foreign reporters to witness the destruction. Picasso later immortalised the atrocity in his well-known painting.

In late August the Italians negotiated a surrender with the Basques, under which leading Basque political figures were to leave the port of Santoña on board two British ships. However as they left port Franco ordered that Nationalist ships blockade the two vessels and then demanded that the prisoners be handed over. Eventually after a stand-off lasting several days the Italians reluctantly agreed. The Nationalists arranged summary trials after which hundreds were shot. Not for the first time in the civil war the Italians were appalled at Franco's behaviour towards his own people. Gradually, however, the Nationalists were able to mop up the rest of northern Spain, including the key mining area of Asturias in the autumn.

Much of the victory in the north was achieved without General Mola, who had been killed in a plane crash on 3 June. Though Franco's power was under little threat, the accident meant that the last of his serious rivals

The ruins of the town of Guernica after being bombed by the German Condor legion

had gone, as so many others had disappeared before. The Caudillo was extraordinarily lucky in the way so many potential contenders for power fell permanently by the wayside. Franco, who was capable of shedding tears at a leaving party, but who was icily cold at times of real tragedy, was unmoved by news of the death of his old colleague. The only moment of unscripted emotion came at Mola's funeral when the increasingly tubby Franco gave a fascist salute and split open his over-stretched uniform, to the discreet mirth of onlookers.

By now, with the north under their control, the Civil War looked to be slowly but inexorably going the Nationalists' way. The only questions were how long the Republicans could cling on in their ever-decreasing territory and whether international events might yet intervene. A few members of the

Franco with his daughter Nenuca in 1938

government in Valencia forlornly hoped they could survive long enough to see the start of the anticipated European war in which they might be saved by French and British intervention. Moreover, one unexpected counterattack masterminded by Vicente Rojo at the village of Brunete west of Madrid did cause Franco to panic momentarily. Ultimately however the attack was beaten back and the Republicans lost 20,000 of their best men. There was a similar outcome in December 1937 when the Republicans broke through at Teruel, only for Franco's troops to destroy important sections of the Republican army by the following February. Franco, who had set up his base in yet another palace, this time the impressive Palacio Muguiro in Burgos, was slowly annihilating the enemy, apparently unfazed by the loss of men and materials it cost his own army. The Generalísimo was in fact capable of quite extraordinary detachment from death. Once when asked about the fate of someone in the Civil War Franco replied that the *Nationalists had him shot* as if were describing events in another country or far in the past.[49]

An early glimpse of how Franco's Spain might look after the war came in January 1938 with the announcement of his first Cabinet. As Minister of the Interior Ramón Serrano Suñer was the dominant figure in a government that carefully reflected Franco's policy of balancing the competing demands of the military, the Falange, the Carlists and other monarchists. Meanwhile Franco himself was busily entertaining diplomatic visitors.

The British agent Sir Robert Hodgson seems to have found the overweight, short and greying Caudillo an attractive character. 'His charm lies in his eyes, which are of a yellowy brown, intelligent, vivacious, and have a marked kindliness of expression'. Franco's eyes were the feature that always caught people's attention; their size and colour plus the length of his eyelashes lent the Caudillo a slightly feminine look. It was also one of the many paradoxes of Franco that visitors often remarked on his politeness, friendliness, even his 'kindliness'. Yet with colleagues and friends he could be haughty, aloof, cool and distant. Once he became the Nationalists' leader even his closest friends had to use the polite 'su' form in Spanish to address him, rather than the more intimate 'tu' form. Friends who had known him since childhood days would not now dare even to pat Franco on the shoulder. However, strictly in private, at least one military colleague referred to the bulky Caudillo as 'fatty' Franco while another colleague likened his high-pitched voice to that of his daughter's, Nenuca.[50]

Even though the Nationalists seemed certain of victory, Franco continued to frustrate both his own officers and the German and Italians with his caution and with his obsession with conquering every inch of territory. He was not remotely interested in a Republican surrender that would leave parts of the country untouched by his own 'cleansing' troops. After a successful offensive in March 1938 towards the north east it looked as if Barcelona and the rest of Catalonia was ready to be taken. Yet the Caudillo pulled back and instead switched the attack to the east and south, possibly nervous that as the European crisis worsened, France might finally be provoked into joining the war on her own doorstep.

The Italians and Franco's own officers were aghast. Even the Republicans were astonished and later claimed Franco could have won the war then had he continued. The volatile Yague, who had spearheaded the attack, was so angry that he publicly berated the decision and also called for a degree of forgiveness after the war and praised the bravery of Republican soldiers. Franco, for whom the language of healing was anathema, and who hated insubordination just as much, relieved Yague of his command, though he later reinstated his old *Africanista* colleague. Meanwhile the Caudillo's later justification for changing the direction of the attack was typical. *I've never played a card without seeing what came next and at that moment I couldn't see the next card.*[51]

Franco savoured a rather more agreeable experience in Burgos on 18 July when the Nationalists celebrated the second anniversary of the uprising. The Caudillo loved anniversaries and ceremonies and revelled in titles and the paraphernalia of office. He was thus delighted when during a ceremony, and surrounded by giant obelisks and huge portraits of himself, the grateful Nationalists officially named Franco Captain–General of the Army and Navy. This was a title that had previously been bestowed only on Spanish monarchs and increased Franco's sense of his own destiny. It also entitled him to fulfil a childhood dream of wearing an admiral's uniform, a dream he would now regularly indulge.

Back in the war, Franco had to endure one more military setback before victory was his. On 25 July the Republicans launched a desperate counter-attack across the River Ebro and caught the Nationalists off guard. The

Franco photographed as the head of the Nationalist navy in the uniform of the Admiral of the Fleet

result was a battle that lasted for four months and caused huge casualties on both sides. Eventually sheer force of numbers and superior supplies meant that the Nationalists were able to stage their own counter-attack and virtually annihilate the Republican army, which ultimately lost nearly 15,000 soldiers. The battle of Ebro caused consternation among his own officer corps, and there were heated arguments about the conduct of the war. It also infuriated Franco's German and Italian allies. An aggrieved Mussolini raged: 'Either the man doesn't know how to make war or he doesn't want to. The reds [Republicans] are fighters, Franco is not.'[52]

During the bloody attrition of Ebro, Franco also began to worry that the worsening crisis in Europe could yet affect his conquest of Spain. The Caudillo feared that the situation over the Sudetenland in September 1938 could provoke a conflict in which Britain and France would take action against the Nationalists' over-stretched positions in the Mediterranean, Africa and north–east Spain. Franco's hypocritical response was personally to assure Sir Robert Hodgson of his *warmest feelings of sympathy for England*.[53] He then informed Rome and Berlin that, due to Spain's weakness and despite his natural inclinations to do so, Spain would not be able to side with them in any war and would remain neutral.

Hitler was disgusted and disdainful, Mussolini incandescent with rage, especially as he still had 40,000 Italian troops in Spain fighting for the Nationalists. It was an example of how fickle and flexible Franco was prepared to be to preserve his position of power. Once it was clear that Britain was not prepared to go to war with Germany over Czechoslovakia Franco wasted no time in sending personal messages of congratulation to Hitler for his international triumph. In future years the cornerstone of Franco's foreign policy would be based on telling different stories about Spain's intentions according to whom he was dealing with.

With the end of the war at last in sight, Franco's brother Ramón was killed during a flying mission over the Mediterranean on 28 October. His body was later found floating in the sea. Franco had long been alienated from his younger brother, though Ramón had eventually renounced his radical Republican past and had joined the Nationalist cause after the start of the Civil War. Based in Mallorca, Ramón had been on a Nationalist bombing raid aimed at Valencia when his plane crashed in poor weather. When told the news, Franco reacted with his usual coolness. Though he must have felt some loss at the death of a brother, he barely showed it. Franco sent a telegram to the Air Force stating that *it is nothing to give a life joyfully for the Patria* though he also wrote of his pride that the *blood of my brother, the aviator Franco* was being united with other fallen airmen. This rather impersonal tribute was followed by a lavish funeral in Mallorca, which Franco did not attend. Instead he sent his older elder brother Nicolás to represent him. Later Franco would further demonstrate his remarkable capacity for coldness by virtually ignoring the existence of his younger brother's widow and daughter.[54]

The final phase of the war began in late December 1938 when, after some trademark hesitation, Franco agreed to a full-scale assault on Catalonia with the help of Italian forces. By the middle of January Tarragona had fallen and finally on 26 January Nationalists entered a silent and starving Barcelona. As was commonplace after Nationalist victories anyone with Republican sympathies was rounded up and thousands were summarily executed.

In the build up to this vital attack Franco still found time to attend to personal interests. Two supporters in Galicia had started a public subscription in which local people could show their financial appreciation of their local 'hero'. How many gave willingly and how many felt obliged to donate cannot be known, but the result was enough money to buy Franco an impressive and restored country residence near La Coruña. On 5 December Franco himself travelled to pick up the keys to the property. The two organisers were later rewarded with well-paid jobs in the Franco regime. In Africa Franco had been content to put up with the heat, dust and dirt of army life. Increasingly however he began to enjoy the very comfortable surroundings that his new position brought him.

As well as future comforts, Franco was also turning his thoughts to post-Civil War Spain. In an end of year interview Franco again ruled out any kind of reconciliation after the war, a promise he would emphatically keep. On 13 February 1939 Franco established the Law of Responsibilities, retroactive to October 1934, in which people who had merely supported the Republic were deemed guilty of a crime, punishable by the severest penalties. Simply showing 'serious passivity' would be deemed as support of the Republic. In effect the Nationalists could and would punish anyone

Nationalists unloading arms

they chose. More fancifully, and echoing the kind of rhetoric used by his friends in Berlin and Rome, Franco held out a vision of a new Spanish empire. He threw out a barely disguised warning to Britain and France against *efforts to reduce Spain to slavery in the Mediterranean.*[53]

In Spain itself Franco was on the verge of his total victory. The fall of Catalonia had marked the real end of military resistance and by early February 1939 the divided Republican government had utterly crumbled. President Azaña fled to France, followed by Juan Negrín, Prime Minister since May 1937, and even General Vicente Rojo. Meanwhile in Madrid there was a brief civil war within a civil war as a Republican military junta arrested communists. Still Franco refused any suggestion of a conditional surrender or conditional peace. Eventually, leaderless and hopeless, the vast majority of the remaining Republican soldiers quietly left their posts and either surrendered or tried to make their way back home. The Nationalist advance eastwards on 26 March was less an attack than a procession through undefended positions. By 27 March a quiet Madrid had been occupied and four days later all of Spain was finally in nationalist hands. The usually robustly healthy Franco was ill in bed with a fever on the very day of his ultimate triumph. However he was well enough to scribble a final bulletin on the progress of the war. Issue on 1 April 1939 it read simply: *On this day, with the red army captive and disarmed, the Nationalist troops have attained their final military objectives. The war has ended.*[bd] In fact, as Republican Spain was about the find out, this was not entirely true. For as far as Franco was concerned the war against the 'enemies' of Spain would never really be over.

Peace but no Reconciliation 1939-1940

Franco's victory in April 1939 had brought order to Spain but at a huge price. The exact number of people killed during the Civil War remains unclear and is still a controversial subject. However it is accepted by many that the overall death toll, including combat deaths, executions, disease and malnutrition was around 500,000. In addition tens of thousands of Republican Spaniards also chose permanent exile rather than face almost certain imprisonment or execution. Franco showed little sign of remorse for the huge loss of life caused by the civil war.

Indeed, the killing continued. Thousands of Republicans or anyone suspected of being a Republican were rounded up and punished. One detailed study suggests that there were nearly 28,000 political executions between 1939 and 1945. Many more were imprisoned – there were 250,000 prisoners in Spanish jails in early 1940 – and often put to work as penal labour. Penal labour was important for Franco. Though he recognised the need to remove the *hatred and passions* of the war, this had to be done not with *liberal* amnesties which were a *deception*. Instead the removal of the hatred had to be achieved on Christian lines *by means of redemption through work accompanied by repentance and penitence.* The post-war peace was to be based absolutely on the victorious side's terms.[57]

Franco himself displayed a level of triumphalism befitting someone who has saved the Fatherland from outside attack; indeed as far as the Caudillo was concerned this was precisely what he had done. A series of victory parades were held in April and May in a number of provincial cities, for example Valencia, in which Italian and German troops also took part. The culmination came on 18 May when Franco finally made his entry into Madrid, the city that he had tried to capture for nearly three years. The city was decked out in yellow and red Nationalist colours as the victorious

Franco viewed the victory march in Madrid from an elaborate tribune. April 1939

Caudillo rode through the streets – one of them already named after him – on his trademark white horse.

The next day a proud Franco looked on as no fewer than 200,000 troops and militia, including Italian Black Shirts, Falangist and Carlist militiamen and Moorish mercenaries marched past him. The procession was nearly sixteen miles long and took five long hours to pass, but it was just the kind of ceremony the Generalísimo adored. There was yet more to come. A *Te Deum* service was held at the basilica of Santa Barbara in Madrid in praise of the Nationalists' victory at which the link between Franco and Spain's past military warrior heroes such as El Cid was made explicit.

The support of the Church was important both to Franco and his new regime. Apart from a few years in his early days as a soldier, Franco was a conventionally devout Catholic, influenced first by his mother and then by his wife Carmen. Franco saw the Church as one of the cornerstones of Spain both past and present. The fact that during Second Republic the government had tried to curb the influence of the Church, and that many priests were murdered during the Civil War, only strengthened this conviction.

Franco was therefore delighted when as early as 3 April Cardinal Gomá had written to him saying: 'God has found in Your Excellency the worthy instrument of his providential plans.' Soon afterwards Pope Pius XII praised the new Spanish leader for his 'most noble and Christian sentiments'.[58]

Indeed, as Franco started to fashion his new Spain out of the wreckage of the Civil War, the Church once more played a central role in the state. This was despite the fact that church attendance before the conflict had been among the lowest in Christian Europe. Perhaps fewer than 20 per cent of people regularly went to mass, while in Easter 1936 only 16 per cent of the population fulfilled their pious duties as Catholics. Now however under Franco the Church was to play a key role as the guardian of the nation's morals and regain its crucial influence over education.

Rodrigo Díaz de Vivar (1040–1099), better known to history was El Cid ('lord' or 'the Boss' in Arabic) is one of the heroic figures of Spanish history. He is regarded as a great warlord and leader and was often held up by the Nationalists as a symbol of the centuries-long fight by Christian Spain to remove the Moors from the peninsula; Franco identified with this role, though in his case the 'enemy' were communists, socialists, freemasons and democrats. In fact, El Cid was a mercenary, albeit one with chivalrous qualities, who fought both against and for Muslim leaders at different times.

Some of the 17,000 Italian troops that marched at the head of the victory procession

Franco's Spain was indeed profoundly conservative. Republican laws allowing divorce in certain circumstances were removed, meaning that once again an annulment was the only way for a marriage to end, apart from death. The naturally conservative Franco doubtless felt that such a measure

was right in principle, but may also have been influenced by his mother's very traditional attitude towards marriage, one which contrasted so greatly with his father's. The legal penalties for abortion were also increased and women's rights were restricted generally. For example, a woman could not open a bank account or take a job without her husband's consent.

In the countryside the limited land reforms of the Second Republic were also scrapped. Meanwhile tight censorship controlled not just the politics of the press but also ensured that the regime's views on morality, nationalism and international politics were maintained. Franco's anti-communist fanaticism was reflected in the fact that Russian salad had to be re-named as either 'national' or 'imperial' salad, Leningrad had to be referred to as St Petersburg and the International Red Cross was considered virtually a communist organisation. Even the seemingly harmless story of *Little Red Riding Hood* had its colour changed to blue because of the associations between 'red' and communism. At the same time, not only were the orphans of dead Republicans forced to be baptized and given new identities but in some cases children were reportedly taken from left-wing opponents and either placed into convents and monasteries or put into Nationalist homes. In addition, attempts by the Catalans and the Basques to express their own identity were repressed. Franco's desire to 'cleanse' Spain touched all corners of society.

The Catholic Church long had a central role in Spanish society. Its identification with the Reconquest of Christian Spain from the Islamic Moors from the 8th to the late 15th century left it closely associated with Spanish nationalism and self-identity. The work of the Spanish Inquisition further increased its status and helped reduce any religious or cultural opposition. However, the Church's links with the state, and its status as a landowner, meant its was increasingly seen as an enemy by those who wanted reform and a fairer Spain. Thus anti-clericalism was a powerful theme of the Second Republic.

The opposition to Franco and the Nationalists was practically extinguished by the three years of civil war, though some guerrilla resistance did continue until the early 1950's. Made weary, hungry and ill by war, much of Republican Spain had little stomach left for a fight against Franco's state, the growing power of the church, the far-reaching bureaucracy of the new combined FET y de las JONS party and the ever-vigilant army. Even the widespread hunger and poverty among Spaniards failed to result in much unrest.

In fact, Franco's biggest headache was how to handle the very different strands of opinion that made up the political Right. They had all supported the Nationalist cause against the Republicans, but now the fighting was over their agendas which were very different. These ranged from militant Catholics, through Falangists who wanted a one-party fascist-style state, to monarchists. Many in the army particularly wanted a quick return of a king; some even looked to the British system of a democratic monarchy as an ideal model.

Franco was generally very adept at balancing these competing interests. He allowed them to squabble between each other while appearing detached from the process; yet simultaneously in private Franco persuaded each of the groups that they were his favourite. This success is often attributed to his famous *gallego* cunning. Meanwhile everyone on the right knew that they owed their victory to Franco. He was able to hint that without him in power the old chaos of the past would return. In this way the tensions within the Right in Spain helped maintain Franco's grip on power. The Caudillo's awareness of this perpetual juggling act was reflected even in the clothes he wore. During the victory parade of 19 May 1939 Franco donned military khaki, but also added a blue shirt in recognition of the Falangists, and the red beret as a nod towards the Carlists.

The question of regional autonomy for the Catalans and Basques had been a divisive one in Spain for many years. For many in the army, Franco included, any degree of autonomy constituted the break up of the Fatherland and was a betrayal of Spain. Thus the Franco regime not only repealed the self-government laws passed by the Republicans, it also sought to suppress all expression of regional identity. The Basque and Catalan languages were banned and the folk music and dance typical of those areas proscribed. Parents were even forbidden from christening their children with any names other than the Spanish (Castilian) names set out in the calendar of saints.

The hue of Franco's regime also changed according to prevailing international conditions. While the Axis Powers of Germany and Italy were in the ascendant Franco's regime was as close as it ever got to becoming a fascist state – semi-fascism as it has been called. Later, it would cloak itself

A smiling Franco now installed as the ruler of Spain–

in slightly more democratic and technocratic clothes, though it would always remain authoritarian. More immediately, when Franco announced his new Cabinet on 9 August 1939 it reflected the same careful balance of monarchists and Falangists, and of pro-Axis and pro-Allied personalities.

Before announcing the Cabinet, Franco made it clear where the real power lay, and that was with him. Though the Caudillo had mostly admired the dictatorship of Miguel Primo de Rivera he felt that the general's biggest mistake was not to institutionalise his powers. Franco did not make the same mistake. On 8 August Franco signed a law giving him massive powers. It meant that he could, in urgent situations, make or unmake a law without a reference to any administrative or legislative body, including the Cabinet. These were effectively the powers of a medieval king.

In fact, Franco was beginning to behave in a quasi-regal manner, as if he really were the king of Spain and his wife Carmen his queen. The former hero of Africa had grown to revel in his new lifestyle and this was shown not just in his expanding waistline but also in his choice of residence.

Even during the Civil War Franco had set up residence in provincial palaces, and now the war was over he was not minded to settle for anything less than the best. This is why when he finally moved his headquarters from Burgos to Madrid in October his initial preference was for the magnificent Palacio de Oriente, the royal palace. The 18th century building boasts 240 balconies, and 44 sets of stairs and was the traditional residence of the Bourbon dynasty. The choice of such a symbolic and opulent building horrified Franco's main adviser Serrano Súñer. Serrano knew that at a time of widespread poverty and hunger in Spain, such a move would send out a very bad signal to the country. Moreover, if Franco moved into the royal palace it would tell the monarchists that Franco had no real intention of restoring the monarchy and thus undermine his critical political balancing act.

Eventually Franco agreed with his brother-in-law and chose the less ostentatious palace of El Pardo, just outside Madrid, which was originally a royal hunting lodge. For Franco and Carmen its main attractions were its regal connections and the fact that it was secluded. An additional attraction for Franco was that it also had an estate in which he could indulge one of his great pastimes, hunting.

Before they could move into El Pardo it needed modernising and so Franco and Carmen moved temporarily into the castle of Viñuelas, twelve miles outside the capital. While he was making his new palatial home fit for a Caudillo, Franco was also sorting out the salary he would receive as head of state. The sum agreed was an annual 700,000 pesetas. This would equate to a salary of more than £600,000 at the start of the 21st century, and did not include the money he received for his other positions such as being head of the armed forces and the FET y de las JONS. In all Franco and Carmen would acquire more than 15 properties in their lifetime, including a mansion and estate near El Escorial, while the acquisitive Carmen owned an entire apartment building in Madrid. It has also been estimated that

A view of the entrance to the vast monument to the victims of the civil war

Franco received around £4million worth of gifts while he ruled Spain.[59]

Though Franco did not take over the royal palace, this did not prevent he and Carmen acquiring regal airs and graces. On great religious ceremonial occasions Franco would make a point of occupying the seat traditionally reserved for Spain's monarchs. He also insisted that Carmen be referred to as '*la Senora*' ('Ma'am'), the usual address for the aristocracy and that the Royal March be played whenever she appeared at a state function. Franco made sure Carmen was treated with the respect she merited as the wife of the saviour of Spain.

Franco's love of pageantry and his subtle understanding of the value of presentation were shown once again on 20 November 1939. This was the third anniversary of the execution of José Antonio Primo de Rivera the former leader of the Falange. Franco had not liked Primo, and had done little to help the young man get out of prison, as he had for other prominent Nationalists in the Civil War. The Caudillo became irritated whenever the late Falange leader was spoken of in flattering terms. He once snapped at Serrano – a friend of José's – for *always going on about that lad as if he was something out of the ordinary.*[60] Yet the Generalísimo also recognised the importance of José – now that he was safely dead – as a symbol of the Falange and one that he, Franco, could channel to his own ends.

Accordingly the regime organised a massive ceremony in which José's body was exhumed from its resting place in Alicante and taken by a series of torchlight processions to El Escorial, near Madrid, the traditional resting place of the monarchs of Spain. Here Primo was buried amid considerable ceremony. Representatives from Germany and Italy were present, together with personal wreaths from Mussolini and Hitler. Franco was able to use this event to cement his position as the inheritor of the Falangist mantle in Spain. It was also an occasion for more blood-letting. The anger of the Falangists at their late hero's execution led to a mob of them storming the prison in Alicante and slaughtering a number of Republican prisoners.

Franco's next grandiose project showed emphatically how he viewed his place in Spain's history. The Caudillo wanted to build something that would stand as an eternal monument to his greatness. On 1 April 1940, the first anniversary of the end of the Civil War, he announced plans for a huge monument to be built at the valley of Cuelgamuros, not far from El Escorial. It would be known as the Valley of the Fallen (*valle de los Caidos*). Although in theory a memorial for all victims of the Civil War, it was in effect a monument to the Nationalist victory. Referring to his *Crusade*, Franco's official decree declared : *The stones to be erected must have the grandeur of the monuments of old, which defy time and forgetfulness...* Franco himself took a very close interest in the work, which would take 20

The interior of the mausoleum at the Valley of the fallen

years to complete. He chose the site himself and sketched out rough plans for the basilica – to be hewn out of solid rock – and huge towering cross that he wanted built. He also set off the first charge of dynamite. Many have said that the project was the nearest thing that Franco ever came to having 'another woman'.[61] As an added twist, the manual labour at this vast and expensive tribute to fallen nationalists was carried out by defeated Republican prisoners, many of whom were injured, fell ill or even died during the construction work.

Franco also wanted more practical signs of Spain's renewed greatness in the form of an empire. As we have seen, the demise of Spain's once-massive empire in the 19th century, culminating in the loss of Cuba in 1898, was a powerful grievance for many military men such as Franco. His own experiences in the country's last remnants of empire in Morocco had shown Franco where he believed Spain's imperial destiny lay – in Africa and the Mediterranean. The Caudillo was also very aware of the imperial ambitions of his Axis friends Mussolini and Hitler, and felt that what was good enough for them was good enough for Spain. In the early hours of 14 June 1940 Spanish troops occupied the North African city of Tangier, which had previously been under international administration. It was a bold gesture, admired even by Hitler, and Franco saw it as the start of a new era of Spanish imperialism. Yet it was the only real step that Spain would ever make towards Franco's dream.

One reason why a Spanish empire was unthinkable at the end of the 1930's was the state of the army. After the shattering experience of the Civil War, the army was in poor shape. Though a large number of soldiers were kept on duty, and military spending took up a third of the national budget – taking away valuable resource from a stricken economy – Spain was barely able to defend itself let alone launch a significant foreign expedition. The wider economy too was a mess; there was a shortage of food, much of the nation's industry was in ruins, unemployment was high and a flourishing black market once more accentuated the differences between rich and poor.

Yet the main reason why Franco's imperial hopes were doomed from the start was the advent of the Second World War and the Caudillo's utterly parochial view of what this might mean for Spain. Franco hoped that Germany's initial successes in the war would enable Spain to carve out an empire from the wreckage of France's overseas territories. This included the majority of Morocco. He assumed that all he needed to do was pledge Spain's support for Hitler, in return for which the new colonies would fall into his lap.

However, Franco never really understood Hitler's strategic thinking. He failed to grasp that Spain, feeble militarily and economically, had little to offer a powerful Germany, or that Berlin might have its own designs on an African empire. He did not realise that Germany had little cause to offer Madrid anything when it could receive so little in return. Indeed the two main benefits that Spain was able to give Germany – the valuable mineral wolfram used in armaments and providing a base for submarines – Berlin

An aerial view of the complex at the Valley of the fallen after its completion

was able to get without the need to offer any colonial possessions in return. When it came to bargaining for empire with a rampant Germany, Franco's hand was pitifully weak.

Franco's inability to grasp the wider picture possibly stemmed from his remote style of rule. He and Carmen spent most of their time in the seclusion of El Pardo, where Franco not only lived but also held his Friday Cabinet meetings and received visitors. The main reasons for him leaving were to go shooting, which was becoming almost an obsession. Curiously, in 1940, one of the most dramatic and uncertain periods of European history, Spain's new leader also found another hobby, that of painting. Franco had shown some inclination towards drawing in his youth. His new-found interest in painting came while he was posing for a portrait and the artist had forgotten to clear away his materials one day. Franco had a go himself and became hooked. However, his main quality as an artist was said to be 'tenacity rather than talent'.[62]

As well as being distracted by his hobbies, the Caudillo seemed dangerously convinced of his own insular analysis of the world situation. Sir Samuel Hoare, the British Ambassador to Madrid, who noted that Franco's writing desk gave pride of place to signed photographs of Mussolini and Hitler, said it was hard to break through the Spanish leader's 'amazing complacency.' He also wondered how this small 'corpulent, bourgeois' figure with a voice like that of a 'doctor with a big family practice and an assured income' could ever have been a war hero in Africa and the leader in a bloody civil war.[63]

One of Sir Samuel's main tasks was to make sure Spain remained neutral in the war. Franco had already declared the country's neutrality on 4 September, almost immediately after the outbreak of hostilities. Given the pitiful state of Spain's army, he had little choice. But it was always clear where Franco's real loyalties lay, and they were not with what he saw as the weak, freemason-dominated democracies of countries such as Britain. In June 1940, for example, when German troops were sweeping all before them in Europe, he sent a personal letter to Hitler that typified his real views. He stated: *At the moment when the German armies, under your leadership, are bringing the greatest battle in history to a victorious close, I would like to express to you my admiration and enthusiasm and that of my people, who are watching with deep emotion the glorious course of a struggle which they regard as their own.* At the same time Franco asked for Hitler's understanding as to why, because of her economic problems and her fear of the British Navy, Spain could not at the moment join sides with Germany.[64]

Soon after writing this letter Franco announced that Spain was changing its status in the war from that of neutrality to 'non belligerence', and within a short time Franco's men had occupied Tangier. The Allies feared this was a prelude to Spain joining the war on the Axis side. First however, Franco needed to send Hitler his shopping lists of demands in return for Spain's participation. This was the prelude to Franco's historic face-to-face encounter with the German leader to decide on Spain's role in World War Two.

Staying Out of the War 1940-45

In the summer of 1940 it looked as if the European War was about to end with a crushing German victory. France had fallen and Britain, despite the heroism of the RAF, seemed next on the list of Germany's conquests. That was certainly the view of Franco, who had watched Hitler's military successes with admiration and was eager that Spain should join in on the winning side. But his natural caution and hope for a Spanish empire led Franco to tread warily. On 18 June he presented Berlin with a list of conditions in return for joining the Nazi war effort. They included receiving a large slice of North Africa, currently under the control of conquered Vichy France, and enough economic and military aid to allow Spain to take part in the war.

For Hitler the demands were extraordinary. First, German aid had already helped Franco win the Spanish Civil War. Secondly, the German army was currently flattening all before it without any obvious need for whatever the Spanish army might offer. Politically, Hitler did not want to alienate Marshal Henri Pétain's tame Vichy regime in France over North Africa, nor risk a joint Anglo-Free French incursion in North Africa. Finally, Hitler had plans for his own bases in Morocco and hankered after one of the strategically valuable Canary Islands.

The Fuhrer's public reaction was non-committal rather than hostile. Yet after Serrano Súñer had travelled to Berlin to meet the German foreign minister Joachim von Ribbentrop to reiterate the Spanish terms, the Fuhrer was privately scathing about Franco's cheek. In particular he wondered witheringly whether Spain had the 'same intensity of will for giving as for taking'.[65]

For his part Franco was dismayed at the Germans' reaction to his conditions and their own tough counter demands. Naively the Caudillo chose to believe this was the fault of the Fuhrer's henchmen, rather than of Hitler himself. Indeed his admiration for the German leader remained undiminished. In July 1940 Franco told the Portuguese ambassador, with apparent sincerity, that he considered Hitler to be an *extraordinary man, moderate, sensitive, full of the spirit of humanity and with great ideas.* On 17th July Franco gave an aggressive and at times anti-Semitic speech in which he spoke of Spanish designs on Gibraltar and in Africa. The Caudillo also spoke threateningly of Spain's *two million warriors ready to fight in defence of our rights* and praised the discipline and unity that had led the Fuhrer to his *fantastic victories on the field of Europe.*[66] Franco loved receiving medals and awards, and was therefore delighted when the day after this belligerent speech Hitler bestowed on him the Grand Cross of Gold of the Order of the German Eagle. It was the highest award Germany could give to a foreign national.

Franco's confidence in the Axis' ultimate victory was reflected in the offhand way he treated both the US and British ambassadors. He cancelled scheduled meetings with the US's Alexander Waddell without warning, and alternated between a swaggering boastfulness and an icy coolness towards the UK's Sir Samuel Hoare. Yet despite such behaviour, which bordered on the childish, Franco was still aware of the real problems his country faced. Spain desperately lacked basic raw materials and given Germany's evident reluctance to lavish more aid on Madrid, an unabashed Franco signed a commercial agreement with Britain and Portugal in July 1940. Then in September he asked the US for a massive credit to fund the purchase of essential items such as fuel. For their part the Allies ignored most of the slights and the virulently anti-democratic rhetoric in order to pursue their own aims.

The regime's erratic diplomatic posturing was not just a sign of Spain's desperate state but also of the ultra-cautious Franco's reluctance to commit himself irrevocably to one side or to one course of action. Nonetheless the meeting between Franco and Hitler seemed to be a stepping-stone for Spain's imminent entry into the war. The encounter was scheduled for 23 October 1940 in the French border town of Hendaye. For Franco the meeting was an attempt to get the best possible deal in return for joining a war he was still convinced the Axis would win, even if British stubbornness now seemed likely to extend it. Hitler, however, was far more circumspect. His aim was to assess whether it was worth Spain joining the war or, as he suspected, Germany would be better served by keeping Vichy France on side by refusing to hand over parts of French North Africa to Franco.

On a personal level the meeting was a failure, though it was later proclaimed a diplomatic triumph by Franco's acolytes. It started badly when, to his acute embarrassment, Franco's rickety train was eight minutes late even though it had very little distance to travel across the border. Meanwhile Hitler, warned in advance not to expect an heroic figure, was deeply unimpressed with Franco. In particular he was driven close to distraction by Franco's 'monotonous' voice as the Caudillo droned on for an hour about the historic destiny of Spain in North Africa. Later Hitler, who described Franco as a 'Latin charlatan' and 'cowardly', said that he would prefer 'having three or four teeth pulled' rather than go through such a meeting again. Indeed at one point, when Franco tactlessly suggested that Britain would continue the war from Canada even if she were invaded, Hitler very nearly walked out of the meeting. His overall view of Franco was that 'there is nothing to be done with this fellow'.[67] Photographs taken at the encounter are also instructive. They show a Franco who is proud to be seen with the German leader, while an expressionless Hitler merely looks as if he would rather be somewhere else.

As the two leaders parted, Franco showed how much the meeting

The main goal of the Allies during the war was to ensure that Spain remained neutral, at virtually any cost. Britain could not afford to have Gibraltar and the entrance to the Mediterranean under German threat if Spain chose to join the Axis war effort. Their tactics were to offer Spain enough of the fuel, food and other raw materials she needed to keep her going without providing enough to rebuild the shattered country. The aid was always conditional on Spain's neutrality and was reduced or even stopped if Franco was deemed to be getting too helpful to the Axis.

The conference at Hendaye was the only occasion when Hitler and Franco met

meant to him when he told Hitler that despite what he had said, *if one day Germany really needed me, she would have me unconditionally at her side without any demands on my part*. Fortunately for the usually wily Franco the interpreter did not translate this naïve final comment. Not long after, however, Franco was himself railing about the Germans,

At Bordighera in Italy, Franco and Serrano Suñer with Mussolini

declaring: *These people are intolerable. They want us to come into the war in exchange for nothing.*[68]

As well as being a personal disaster, the meeting achieved little politically either. The two countries signed a secret protocol that emphasised Spain's intention to enter the war, but at an unspecified time. From that day onwards, and though German and Spanish enthusiasm for Madrid's entry into the war waxed and waned, there was little real prospect of Franco entering the war directly, even if there was a widespread assumption in Madrid immediately after the meeting that war was imminent.

His supporters would later claim that it was Franco's brilliant diplomacy that had kept Spain out of the war. This was far from the truth. Franco had wanted to join the war but the conditions were never quite right; this was because for Hitler the limited value of Spain's entry was never worth the concessions he would have to make. Ultimately it suited neither side quite enough to make it happen. This was confirmed when a meeting between Franco and Mussolini in Bordighera in February 1941 ended equally inconclusively. The Italian leader found the episode a waste of time, while German insults about the 'jumped up, 'arrogant' and 'stupid' Caudillo increased.[69]

At home domestic concerns had forced Franco to dismiss two of his ministers. One, the old *Africanista* Juan Yague, who was strongly pro-Axis and had always been unhappy with Spain's neutral status, was removed for criticizing the regime's lack of concrete support for Germany. Meanwhile the foreign minister Juan Beigbeder was replaced by Serrano Súñer because of his unreliability and his penchant for attractive women, one of whom was suspected of being a British spy. These were reminders that international divisions were reflected even in Franco's own Cabinet.

Yet during these momentous times Franco still had time for other, more curious projects. One was his support for the bizarre suggestion that Spain's serious food shortage could be solved by feeding people with dolphin sandwiches, the bread to be made from fish meal. Like other wild ideas Franco chose to believe in, it came to nothing. Franco's occasional and curious gullibility – which contrasted with his usual caution – was also shown by his excited acceptance of unfounded claims that Spain had huge gold deposits, and of impractical and in one case fraudulent schemes to make synthetic fuel.

Even more remarkably, Franco found time during the winter of 1940/41 to write a novel called Race (*Raza*) which was made into a movie. This curious work was thinly-disguised autobiography and its main protagonists,

Don Juan de Bourbon, the man who should have been king, with his family

the Churruca family, bore a strong resemblance to the Francos. However, in this fantasy version the father was not a womaniser, and significantly their social status was higher than the real-life Franco family. The hero of the plot is José Churruca whose far-sighted father predicts will be either 'a great soldier or a saint'.[70] In the end José becomes an officer in the Nationalist cause and bravely fights to save his country from disaster. This tale shows how simplistically Franco viewed himself and his achievements. Franco wept through much of the film at an early private viewing.

Back in the real world the death of Alfonso XIII at the end of February 1941, a month after he had formally abdicated in favour of his son Don Juan, again pushed the issue of the monarchy to the fore. Many monarchists, including those in the army, were becoming frustrated at

Franco's reluctance to move towards the restoration of the monarchy, and were also angry at the influence of the pro-Falangist Serrano Súñer who was strongly pro-Axis and especially pro-Italy.

Franco was also concerned about his elegant brother-in-law and the following he had among key sections of the Falange. This was around the time when his teenage daughter Nenuca asked one day whether it was 'Papa or Uncle Ramón' who was in charge. There were signs meanwhile that Franco, closeted in El Pardo with Carmen, was getting dangerously isolated from events. The German ambassador noted that 'There is increasing criticism that Franco sees fewer and fewer people and does not allow himself to be advised even by his own friends'.[71]

To reduce the growing tension Franco installed an anti-Falangist, Colonel Valentín Galarza as Minister of the Interior on 5 May 1941 and the malleable José Luis de Arrese, the man behind the dolphin sandwiches scheme, became head of the FET. A further change of Cabinet personnel followed two weeks later. Once more Franco had shown his ability to balance the different factions or 'families' in the regime while maintaining his own grip on power. During the changes Franco had also promoted a naval captain who would eventually become one of the key figures in Franco's Spain, Captain Luis Carrero Blanco.

In June 1941 Hitler's forces invaded the Soviet Union. As a result of his views on communism, Franco had always struggled to accept the opportunistic German-Russian non-aggression pact of 1939. Now that it had been torn up Franco supported the German assault on the home of Marxism with some gusto. He declared that Spain's status was now one

Juan Carlos Teresa Silvestre Alfonso de Borbón (1913-1993) was only the fourth son of Alfonso XIII but was his designated heir. Don Juan spent much of his life in exile, including a spell training in the Royal Navy, and had a difficult relationship with Franco. Neither man liked the other. Don Juan felt Franco denied his rightful place as king of Spain, while Franco viewed the 'soft' Don Juan as dangerously liberal. Ultimately he was never to become king. To Don Juan's profound dismay, his son Juan Carlos was designated as Franco's 'heir'.

Serrano Suñer and the German general Schleier. Paris, 1940

of *moral belligerence* and began to cultivate the theory of 'two wars'. This theory held that there was one war involving Britain and Germany, in which Franco was strictly neutral, and a second war against communism, in which he had a key interest. This was not a distinction that anyone else seriously accepted.[72]

The opening up of the Eastern Front was the closest that Franco and Spain ever got to joining the war. Egged on by excited Falangists and a

Serrano Suñer diatribe against Russia, Franco agreed to send volunteers to help the Germans. The so-called Blue Division entered into combat near Leningrad by the beginning of October. Franco was lucky that Stalin did not retaliate by declaring war on Spain. Meanwhile, still carried away on the tide of pro-German and anti communist rhetoric, Franco made one of his most aggressive speeches yet. On 17 July he bitterly denounced the *age-old enemies of Spain* – Britain France and the United States – and praised Germany for leading a *battle for which Europe and Christianity have for so many years longed...*[73] Even Serrano Súñer and the Axis ambassadors were taken aback by the ferocity of this speech, which deeply angered Britain and the US.

In February 1942 Franco was plunged back into the memories of his real as opposed to his idealised childhood when his father Nicolás died at the age of 84. Franco's father was perhaps the only person in Spain who had been able to get away with publicly insulting the Caudillo. He was often heard in Madrid's bars berating his son, whom he openly described as being 'inept' as well as a 'swine and a pimp'. Such behaviour sometimes led to old Nicolás being arrested, though the embarrassed authorities always released him when they discovered his identity. For his part, Franco had refused to visit his dying father. Perhaps to keep up appearances the Caudillo ordered that a full ceremonial funeral be held, as befitted a man of Nicolás Franco's rank and more pertinently the father of Spain's 'saviour'. The Caudillo, though, did not attend. He also got his revenge on the old man by barring Agustina, his loyal and common law wife of more than 30 years, from the ceremony. His father had loved Agustina and was far happier with her than he had been with his wife, Franco's mother. Franco's spiteful behaviour towards Agustina showed he could be as ruthless with the 'enemy' in his family as he was with the enemies of Spain. Franco also seemed curiously keen to possess his father's old admiral's baton, though in fact this passed to his brother Nicolás.[74]

If Franco's personal life was troubled at this time, then so was the progress of the war. Though the Spanish leader would take some comfort from Allied setbacks in the Far East now that Japan was in the conflict, the situation in

Europe looked increasingly gloomy. Slowly it was becoming clear that the German invasion of the Soviet Union, initially so successful, was stalling in the face of Soviet determination and the unforgiving Russian winter. The long and bloody battle for Stalingrad , which started in the summer of 1942 and ended in crushing German defeat in February 1943, was a turning point. From 1942 onwards and with extreme reluctance, Franco would have to accept that Germany might not win the war, even though right to the end – even after the Normandy landings of 1944 – Franco naively nurtured a hope that Hitler would unleash a secret weapon to sway the outcome. This meant a very gradual and limited thawing of Franco's hitherto icy approach to the Allies.

The shifting fortunes of the war were also reflected in the regime's 'families'. The monarchists, many of whom supported closer co-operation with the Allies, were increasingly open about their dislike for the Falangists, whom they hated for their blind support for the Axis, their anti-monarchism, their all-enveloping political influence and their cynical corruption. The tension came to a head on 16 August 1942 when Falangist supporters threw bombs that injured bystanders at a Carlist church ceremony. Franco now faced one of the worst crises of his time as leader. The anti-Falangist Carlist and Army Minister General Enriquez Varela – who was present at the ceremony – angrily threatened to resign unless strong action was taken against the culprits and their leaders.

Franco's response to this crisis was typical. Having failed to dissuade Varela, he accepted his resignation, and also sacked the Minister of the Interior Garlarza for backing his fellow minister. However, at the beginning of September the Caudillo more than balanced this out by sacking his brother-in-law Serrano Súñer. In doing so Franco had removed the main object of monarchist discontent, while simultaneously maintaining his authority over all the competing parties. It was classic Francoism. So was the Generalísimo's response when Serrano Súñer tried to hand over some final papers to his leader. *I would prefer it if the new minister presented them to me*, said Franco coolly. His supporters later claimed that Franco's dismissal of his pro-Axis brother-in-law was part of a masterly strategy to steer Spain towards the Allies; his replacement General Francisco Gómez Jordana was certainly both relatively neutral and competent. In reality the dismissal was the political price Franco had to pay to maintain his government's stability.[75]

Moreover, it was a price Franco had become increasingly willing to pay for personal reasons too. Franco's envy of the clever, urbane Serrano Súñer was probably sharpened by a doubtless apocryphal story doing the rounds of Madrid concerning Ramon's wife Zita. An old friend who had been abroad for years is said to have congratulated Zita on having married 'the most important man in Spain'. The friend then asked what had happened to her sister Carmen. 'Poor thing,' explained Zita, 'she ended up marrying a soldier'. Meanwhile Franco, who was forgiving about financial corruption but not about sexual indiscretions, was appalled that Serrano Súñer had been having an affair with the wife of an aristocratic soldier. It was perhaps the closest Franco's regime came to a sex scandal and was the talk not just of Madrid society but of the diplomatic corps too.[76]

Franco's response to the shift in the war's direction continued to be a complex and at times contradictory one. This was partly because he himself was split; his heart wanted an Axis victory while his head now saw that the Allies were the likely victors. For example at the start of November 1942, the Spanish leader threatened that any Allied landings in French North Africa would bring Spain into the war on the Axis side. Yet when the landings did occur on 8 November in Operation Torch, Franco did nothing and simply seemed relieved that the Allied forces had not invaded Spain too. On 3 October 1943, meanwhile, Franco switched Spain's formal war status back to neutral even as he continued vital shipments of wolfram to Germany. When the US – which favoured a tougher line with Spain than did Britain – lost patience with the continuing wolfram exports and suspended oil shipments, the embargo hit Spain hard. The most galling result for Franco was that no tanks could take part in the parade of 1 April 1944, the fifth anniversary of the end of the Civil War, because of the fuel shortage.

As the war approached its inevitable conclusion, Franco hoped that small

Vicky's cartoon depicts General Franco, marching out of step, behind the Allies victory parade

changes in his regime - for example the re-establishment of a Parliament (*Cortes*), albeit one with little or no real democratic membership – would allow him entry into the club of the victorious side. He was encouraged by Winston Churchill's recognition in May 1944 that Spain's neutrality had been a contribution to the war effort. However the Caudillo was equally determined that he should not give up the smallest part of his political power. He had not won a bloody civil war and then steered Spain through a world war simply to let someone else take charge. Various attempts by the pretender Don Juan and his monarchist supporters to get Franco to institute a move towards the restoration monarchy were firmly rebuffed.

Don Juan, who had moved steadily towards the Allies since 1942, hoped

that US and British pressure might force Franco's hand. However, he and
his supporters never fully understood that while the Allies may not have
liked Franco's regime, they had no practical reason to change it. A stable,
neutral Spain suited their purpose. On 19 March 1945 a frustrated Don
Juan issued a 'manifesto' from Lausanne in which he claimed that Franco's
regime was 'inspired from its inception by the totalitarian system of the
Axis powers'. Apparently this document 'caused Franco most annoyance
in all his forty years of power'. Franco was worried but also knew that
without direct Allied intervention – which was extremely unlikely – he still
controlled all the levers of power in Spain. Indeed back in October 1944
a small and ill-fated attempt by mostly communist Spanish Republicans
to invade Spain across the Pyrenees gave Franco a great propaganda

opportunity. Inside Spain it allowed Franco to pose as the one person which could keep the country from sliding back to the horrors and chaos of the Civil War years – a prospect few Spaniards could consider without a shudder. Internationally it was an early sign that he could be a useful bulwark against communism. Thus in response to Don Juan's manifesto he was able to respond dismissively to the idea that he should step back and allow a king to become Head of State. *As long as I live I'll never be Queen Mother*, he declared.[77]

Yet despite his justifiable confidence in being able to hold onto power in Spain, Franco's hope that he could play a full part in international affairs were soon disappointed. His decision to break off relations with Japan and Germany in April and May 1945 respectively were tiny gestures compared with the disdain with which much of the world regarded his regime. The vehemence with which he had praised and helped Hitler and Mussolini and insulted the 'corrupt' and 'cowardly' democracies of the West was now reaping its own grim reward. In a vote in June 1945 the new United Nations decided to bar membership to those countries that had been backed by anti-democratic countries whose armies had fought the United Nations. This motion, proposed by Mexico which had become home to thousands of Republican exiles, was aimed specifically at Spain. At home the tightly controlled and sycophantic press might improbably declare the end of the war in Europe to be 'Franco's Victory'. But with his old friends Hitler and Mussolini now dead, and his own regime widely shunned, Franco was about to discover that the outside world was suddenly a very different and lonely place.

Alone 1946-1953

When the Second World War ended Francisco Franco was still in leadership terms a relatively young man at 52. He was younger than both the Soviet leader Joseph Stalin and the new US president Harry S Truman and belonged to almost a different generation from the outgoing British Prime Minister Winston Churchill. Even the new Labour premier Clem Atlee was older by nearly a decade. Yet Franco had already been head of the Nationalist movement for nearly nine years and dictator of Spain for more than six. The years in power had taken their toll on Franco, who had lost all trace of the dashing qualities of his days as a young solider, and had yet to acquire the almost avuncular persona he would have in later life. Instead he looked, as he was, a short, greying, middle-aged man who had put on weight.

There was also something old-fashioned about Franco and his regime. The fascists and Nazis with whom he had been so closely associated were now defeated. After the long years of war, the very idea of a military leader seemed out-dated. The spirit of the age in Western Europe was of civilian governments, social change, the re-building of broken societies and dynamic economies. All this passed Spain and her people by. Franco seemed to symbolise a past that Europe and the rest of the world wanted to forget. For Franco, of course, the world always *would* be stuck in 1936, when he first started his 'crusade' to rid Spain of communism and the folly, as he saw it, of liberal democracy. Franco would go on fighting these demons, real or imaginary, until the bitter end.

The chief victims of Franco's parochial and outdated views were the Spanish people. They had endured the hardships of the Civil War and the deprivations of the Second World War only to find that for them, unlike the rest of Europe, there was no light at the end of the tunnel. Franco took an interest in economics but did not have a sophisticated grasp of the subject. His economic views sprang out of his deeply conservative and nationalist approach to life and the Spanish policy was what is called autarchy. This is an attempt to make a country economically self-sufficient and is a policy often associated with ultra-nationalistic regimes. In Spain's case autarchy turned the country's already fragile economic state into a disaster area. When Franco became head of the Nationalists in 1936 he had pledged that there would be no Spaniard without bread. Yet low wages, unemployment and poverty were the norm; in Spain the 1940's were known as the 'years of hunger'.

When the acclaimed writer Gerald Brenan travelled around Spain in 1949 he found a land of want. Walking the streets of Córdoba he describes how he was 'horrified' by the poverty. 'One sees men and women whose bodies are coated with dirt because they are too weak or too sunk in despair to wash in water. One sees children of ten with wizened faces, women of thirty who are already hags, wearing that frown of anxiety which perpetual hunger and uncertainty about the future give. I have never seen such sheer misery before...[78]

The economic problems were certainly not helped by Spain's pariah status at the end of the war. Thanks to its links with the defeated Axis powers the country was specifically excluded from the massive programme of US funding for Europe known as Marshall Aid. Meanwhile Franco's attitude towards Spain's treatment was typically contradictory and complex. On occasions he raged against foreign Masonic plots that were trying to destroy Spain *because she had carried the gospel to the world.* At other times he tried to show that Spain deserved a place in the international community by re-writing the recent past in the most brazen way. Denying his war-time friendships with Hitler and Mussolini, Franco said in an interview: *It is true that when Germany seemed to be winning the war, some members of the Falange tried to identify Spain with Germany and Italy, but I immediately dismissed all persons so inclined. I never had the slightest intention of taking Spain into the war.* It is even possible that Franco himself had come to believe in this complete distortion of the truth.[79]

In response to the changed world of the post-war era Franco tinkered with the outward appearance of his regime. The role of the Falange was played down while the active participation of the Catholic Church was increased. This was shown in Franco's new cabinet in July 1945 when the prominent Catholic Alberto Martín Artajo became Foreign Minister. The Spaniards' Charter (*Fuero de los Españoles)* in the same year was an attempt to show that all Spaniards had rights in Franco's regime. However, it was a fairly empty charter; the 'rights' were all subject to being compatible with the Franco regime. This was part of what Franco and his apologists called 'organic democracy', which was in reality only marginally organic and not at all democratic.

Despite the gestures, Franco was adamant that he would not share power with anyone else. Nor would he for a second consider standing down even as calls for a return of the monarchy grew. As the Caudillo said with Beckettian brevity and gloom to a senior general: *There will be no resignation. From here only to the cemetery.* Therefore the Spanish leader's reaction was predictable in February 1946 when Don Juan moved base from Switzerland to Estoril in neighbouring Portugal, prompting nearly 500 prominent Spanish monarchists to write a letter of support. Franco wanted them *crushed like worms.* In the event the pro-monarchist General Kindelán, was exiled to the Canary Islands and the Caudillo peevishly cut off all relations with Don Juan for refusing to meet him.[80]

Franco's cosmetic changes to his regime bore little fruit abroad. On 4 March 1946 France, Britain and the US signed a Tripartite Declaration that condemned the Franco regime. France in particular had been angered by the execution of Cristino García, a leader of the continuing anti-Franco guerrilla movement but also a hero of the French Resistance. Franco had characteristically ignored French calls for clemency. Yet the accord also showed how Franco's Spain would one day be rehabilitated in Western eyes. The declaration made it clear that the three powers would not intervene in Spanish internal affairs, their disapproval of its regime notwithstanding. The US especially was worried that Stalin might want to provoke another civil war at a time when communists were starting to come to power in eastern Europe. At this time, too, Winston Churchill made his famous speech about an 'iron curtain' falling across Europe. In a Europe split between communist and democratic regimes, anti-communist Spain would by default join the West.

Soon after this Franco showed a self-pitying quality that sat awkwardly with his image as a strong, confident leader. Opening new rooms at the Military Museum in Madrid the Caudillo declared: *I am the sentry who is never relieved…the one who is watchful while others sleep.* Moreover, he added, the Spanish people should be aware of his self-sacrifices. *I see my private life and my hobbies severely limited; my entire life is work and meditation.* This of course conveniently overlooked his regular pastimes of golf, painting, shooting, fishing, sailing and especially hunting.[81] As ever with Franco, so much was about image and presentation, and manipulating these to his ends. In late 1946, for example, the country was dealt a potentially humiliating blow when the United Nations voted not just to exclude Spain from all UN bodies but also urged all member nations to withdraw their ambassadors from Madrid. In the lead up to this vote, however, protestors held a massive demonstration in the Plaza de Oriente in Madrid. Mobilised by the Falange, hundreds of thousands of Spaniards yelled their support for the Spanish leader, chanting 'Franco yes, communism no' as a beaming Caudillo stood with Carmen on the balcony of the Royal Palace. He cleverly turned the UN's impending vote into a story of a beleaguered Spain fighting bravely against the international forces of freemasonry, communism and foreigners in general. The crowd's biggest cheer came when Franco declaimed that *no one has the right to interfere in the private matters of other nations.*[82] Though it ignored the massive role that Italians and Germans played in Spain both during and after the Civil War it was the kind of rhetoric that struck a chord with many in Spain. The episode also showed the great value of the Falange to Franco domestically, even if it was an embarrassment internationally. The Falange was a mass movement able to conjure up public shows of support.

Another sign of his concern for image – as well as his inflated ego – was his decision to have a new coin minted. On it was an image of Franco and the words: 'Caudillo by the grace of God'.

Despite the Falange's usefulness, Franco felt confident enough in 1947 to risk offending it by making a long-awaited attempt to define the Spanish state. His so-called Law of Succession declared that Spain was a kingdom, something the Falange opposed. Franco understood however that the Falange was in a far weaker position than previously. With all possibility of Axis backing gone, it had only one supporter and one source of power – and that was Franco himself. In any case, though Franco's new law made it clear that Spain was a kingdom, there was as yet to be no king. Franco would be Head of State for life with the right to choose his own – royal – successor.

Don Juan was appalled but could do little or nothing to oppose a law which removed his chances of becoming king in the near future, if at all. The law, inevitably, sailed through the Cortes. Indeed so confidant was Franco of his position that on 6 July 1947 he even held a national referendum on it. Using the media he portrayed the vote as a stark choice between supporting a free, Catholic Spain or allowing foreigners and communism to wreck the country. Even so, and allowing for many voting irregularities, the 93 per cent yes vote out of the more than 15 million who voted gave Franco a limited form of popular legitimacy that he had utterly lacked before. In truth, there was nowhere else for most Spaniards to turn.

Though he had few international friends, Franco made the most of them. One was the Argentinian dictator Juan Perón, whose regime, together with that of the Portuguese dictatorship, helped keep an isolated Spain afloat economically. Though even Perón was reluctant to visit Spain himself, in June 1947 the arrival of his glamorous wife Eva – better known as Evita – was greeted with near-hysteria by the Spanish press, with rapture by large crowds and with delighted relief by Franco. Caught up in the emotion, a proud Franco and a fur-coated Evita even gave fascist salutes to Falangist onlookers. In fact the only person who seems to have been less than happy about Evita's visit was Franco's wife. Photographs of Carmen at the time show her stern-faced as, despite her best efforts, she was effortlessly upstaged and out-dressed by the alluring

Eva Perón had spared no expense on her wardrobe during her European tour

Evita. Carmen was good at adopting a regal hauteur on grand occasions, but could not even begin to match the Argentinian's charisma.

Franco's next important meeting was of a very different nature. Don Juan, who had anyway begun to realise that there was no chance of claiming his throne without Franco's approval, had been encouraged by the Americans to seek a rapprochement with the Generalísimo. For his part Franco wanted a hold over Don Juan he currently lacked. It was therefore agreed that the two would meet aboard Franco's yacht *Azor* on 25 August 1948 in the Bay of Biscay. A talkative Franco dominated the meeting, which he had begun sentimentally by weeping. Soon, though, Franco's main goal became apparent. He wanted Don Juan's ten-year-old son Juan Carlos to finish his education in Spain.

Though Don Juan was non-committal about the idea, Franco later leaked the 'fact' that it was going to happen to his compliant press and the Pretender was forced to agree. Franco now had the chance to influence the next generation of Spanish princes, and had out-manoeuvred his main rival as head of state. On 9 November Juan Carlos duly arrived in Spain, where his development was carefully overseen by hand-picked advisers. Franco's most awkward moment during his meeting with Don Juan came when the Pretender asked if it was true that on a recent hunting trip on a royal estate wild goats had been shot with machine guns. Franco meekly conceded that they had, but this had only happened to animals that were already wounded.

The late 1940's and early 1950's saw a gradual relaxation in some of the international attitude towards Spain. This however had nothing to do with the brilliant diplomacy of a Franco who barely disguised his disdain for the liberals, democrats and 'freemasons' of the Western world. Instead the main reason why the US in particular was slowly beginning to soften its stance towards Franco's Spain was the Cold War.

The split between liberal democracies and communist regimes either side of the Iron Curtain meant that Washington needed all the allies it could get. Moreover, Spain, with its position on the gateway to the Mediterranean, lay in a vital strategic position. Franco of course had been singing the anti-communist tune even before the Spanish Civil War. It was his good fortune – or as his supporters claimed his farsightedness – that in a changed world this tune now had a wider and more appreciative audience. The concrete signs of Franco's rehabilitation were a UN vote permitting member states to send ambassadors back to Madrid, a $62.5million American loan for Spain's military and the appointment on 27 December 1950 of Stanton Griffis as the new US ambassador to Spain.

With customary arrogance, Franco looked out from the seclusion of El Pardo and welcomed the world's acceptance that he had been right all along. In his annual end of year broadcast the triumphant leader described how the world, *disabused of its false delusions, turns its eyes to our Fatherland, in the conviction that, above all, right accompanied Spain.* If Spain had any domestic problems, he said, these were because of very low recent rainfall that had harmed agriculture but above all because of the previous *incomprehension* of the world. In defiance of all the evidence of economic misery described by observers such as Gerald Brenan, Franco then gave a glowing end-of-term report about his own internal achievements. *What Spanish regime at any time has been more productive in carrying out its tasks and has created for the Nation, in any respect, wealth comparable to that created up to now?*[83]

Franco had more personal reasons for enjoying 1950 too. Though he was emotionally controlled, even repressed, Franco's love for his daughter was never in doubt. When she was young he had painted rag dolls for her, and more recently painted her portrait, while Franco also took his daughter on some of his interminable hunting trips. Nenuca meanwhile had herself fallen in love and on 10 April was married to Dr Cristóbal Martínez Bordiú, the future Marqués de Villaverde. Franco had already shown in his novel *Raza* how much social status meant to him. It meant perhaps even more to his wife Carmen. The couple also revelled in ceremony and pageantry. The wedding was therefore a lavish affair. It was held in the chapel at El Pardo, and senior diplomats, the cream of Spanish aristocracy and all the Cabinet were all invited. In all, 800 people attended the banquet. At the nuptials Carmen was bedecked in dazzling jewellery while the bridegroom wore the uniform of the Knights of the Holy Sepulchre, with accompanying helmet and sword. Franco wore one of his favourite outfits, that of the Captain-General of the Spanish Armed Forces, and gave his daughter away. However, he made sure that during the ceremony he occupied the place

Nenuca Franco, the Marquésa de Villaverde and three of her children

usually reserved for the monarch. The press dutifully interpreted this as a sign of Franco's unending devotion to his country; the unrelieved sentry still reporting for duty even at his daughter's wedding. The newspapers also helpfully avoided mention of the many expensive gifts given to the happy couple at a time of widespread privation.

Nenuca's marriage to Villaverde does not seem to have always been a happy one. With Franco and Carmen there was never a hint of marital impropriety, though his wife made sure that few pretty younger women attended official receptions just to be sure. In general though her main aim was to shield Franco from people who might ask awkward questions or raise difficult subjects. This would partly account for his growing isolation in later years. The Marqués however had a reputation as a playboy and his marriage to Nenuca more resembled that of Franco's parents than to the Caudillo's. Society gossips considered that his main reason for marrying Nenuca was the opportunity it gave to trade in on the Franco name. It was not only the most powerful name in Spain, but the most lucrative too. However, the couple did have seven children upon whom their grandfather doted.

Once Franco assumed leadership of the Nationalists in 1936 his family started to make full use of their connections. His older brother Nicolás was notorious for the way he tried to cash in on the Franco name, including the sale of letters of introduction to members of government. His name would later be associated with a serious financial scandal in the early 1970s. The Marqués de Villaverde too quickly made use of his wife's name and made considerable sums of money from various ventures, including the importing of scooters from Italy. His nickname was the 'Marqués de Vayavida' (what a life)'.

Though the international mood was moving his way, Franco was far from subtle in his diplomacy. For example, during 1950 and 1951 Franco orchestrated a noisy campaign for the return for Gibraltar to Spain from British hands. His reasoning was that if the world now needed his help, then it had to give him something in return, in this case the Rock that Spain had ceded to Britain in 1713. When Britain opposed Spain's membership of the North Atlantic Treaty Organisation (NATO) an aggrieved Franco responded by organising demonstrations in Barcelona on 19 February 1951 where protestors bayed for the end of British rule. Franco occasionally found it useful to stir up emotions over the Rock as a diversion from tricky domestic issues.

In the early 1950's the biggest domestic issue – and problem – was the economy. The policy of autarchy or self-reliance was a disaster and

Franco had come to accept the need for some change. Thus one of the most significant trends of his Cabinet re-shuffle on 19 July 1951 was the introduction of new faces who were open to a gradual opening of the economy. Franco refused to sack altogether his old friend and architect of autarchy Juan Antonio Suanzes, but shifted him from the Commerce and Industry portfolios. Instead men such as Manuel Arburúa, a professional economist, stepped into his shoes. He also created a new ministry called Information and Tourism, even if censorship carried on exactly as before. Franco took such moves reluctantly in a calculated attempt to please the American administration, whose financial help he needed. For the first time Franco's regime, rather than standing on the sidelines and

Luis Carrero Blanco (1903–1973) had been a career naval officer who moved quietly and effectively up through the ranks of Franco's regime. Uninspiring but solid and with good political antennae, Carrero shared many of the Franco's prejudices about the world, for example on freemasonry. He served Franco loyally for more than 30 years and eventually became prime minister in 1973, though he was assassinated months later. Carrero Blanco's one wobble was in 1950 when there were rumours of problems in his marriage, which briefly threatened his influence with Franco and the ever-vigilant and pious Carmen.

shaking its fist at the world, had given a practical sign of wanting to engage with it. It would however be a slow process. Meanwhile the other significant part of the reshuffle was the appointment to ministerial rank of Luis Carrero Blanco.

If Franco had a stubborn attachment to autarchy, his belief in the evils wrought by freemasonry was even greater. Since 1946 he had written regular articles in the newspaper *Arriba* on the subject. Using the pseudonym Jakim Boor, Franco gave vent to his deep and visceral loathing of freemasons who, along with communists, he blamed for all the world's and especially Spain's problems. These articles were eventually published as a book entitled *Freemasonry (Masonería)* in 1952. It makes strange reading, all the more so when one considers that the author was the head of an important European country. Franco believed that all modern human history had been shaped by masons. Spain was a particular target and had been weakened by freemasonry ever since it was introduced there in 1728 by the British politician Philip, Duke of Wharton, the author claimed. More recently the old League of Nations and the United Nations were international vehicles for Masonic intriguing. Franco further claimed that while Mussolini and Hitler had nobly fought back against the conspiracy, two of the most prominent freemasons had been or were President Roosevelt and Winston Churchill. Franco, in his guise as Jakim Boor, also suggested Roosevelt and Churchill had formed a Masonic/communist pact with the Soviet Union at the end of the Second World War. It is difficult to know what to make of such extraordinary ravings. At the very least they indicate a mind prone to 'obsession' and 'fantasy'.[84] Franco, who had been very aware of his own father's Masonic leanings, certainly had a personal as well as a political hatred of freemasons. There is every reason to believe that Franco, writing in the isolation of El Pardo, believed what he was writing. In Washington, where no one was fooled by the pseudonym, there was considerable irritation. However, personal dislike of Franco, his regime and his views were not to get in the way of the need for Spanish military co-operation as the Cold War became ever more glacial. Indeed US President Harry S Truman was explicit. In July 1951 he told his Chief of Naval Operations: 'I don't like Franco and I never will but I won't let my personal feelings override the convictions of you military men.'[85] The White House's pragmatism paved the way for Franco and his despised regime finally to come in from the international wilderness. That would ultimately help satisfy Franco's and Spain's material needs. However, to satisfy his needs for spiritual approval of his regime, Franco first sought approval from a very different source.

In From the Cold 1953-1962

Francisco Franco did not always have an easy relationship with the Catholic Church. As a young soldier in Africa he had famously been described as 'sin misa' ('without mass'), though later, helped by the dutiful example of Carmen, he had regained his piety. Nor was Franco always respectful of senior church figures. For many years he was plagued by the obdurate Spanish Cardinal Pedro Segura from Seville who bloody-mindedly declined to bend to Franco's every whim. In 1948, for example, the Cardinal refused to allow Carmen to take his place at the head of a table for an official banquet, on the grounds that only monarchs or heads of state had that right. When Franco's officials protested, Segura offered them a choice; a banquet without him, without Carmen or no banquet at all. A furious Franco and Carmen chose the third option.

Nevertheless Catholicism was an essential ingredient of the mixture that made up the Franco regime, even more so since the end of the Second World War. Franco was therefore keen to get public and international recognition from the head of the Catholic Church, the Pope himself. The result, after five years of diplomacy and negotiation, was the signing in August 1953 of an official Concordat with the Vatican. Though this document mostly confirmed existing practice, for Franco it was a massive statement of support for his regime. On another, more personal level too it gave the religious and superstitious Franco a final seal of approval for all the blood he had shed to win power. His 'crusade' had officially won the backing of God's representative on Earth. Soon afterwards Franco gushingly described Spain as *one of the greatest spiritual reserves of the world*. The Caudillo's and Carmen's delight increased further when on 21 December 1953 Pope Pius XII awarded 'our beloved son' the Supreme Order of Christ, the highest distinction the Vatican could award.[86]

Cardinal Tedeschini introduces Monsignor MonZerat to Franco. Barcelona, 1952

The Vatican agreement was helpful in proclaiming Franco's moral rehabilitation in the international community, but it was the 1953 deal with the United States that was to prove of more long-term and tangible benefit. As he had tried to do with Hitler, Franco haggled with the Americans over the price he would get in return for his support. Unlike the German leader, however, the Americans had money to spare and, more importantly, saw a concrete benefit in getting Franco on board. The so-called Pact of Madrid was signed on 26 September 1953 and gave the US the right to build three airbases and one naval base, plus smaller military installations. In return Franco's regime was to receive $226million in military and technological aid.

Franco's agreement with the US demonstrated his acceptance by the world's major power and simultaneously made Spain a more attractive destination for foreign investors. The country already had low wages and abundant labour while strikes were illegal. Now the Spanish state had been given a warranty by the world's leading capitalist. As a result overseas investment would begin to flow into Spain in the late 1950's and early 1960's.

There were however two main drawbacks to the American deal. The first was that handing over military bases to the US compromised Spanish sovereignty, and thus undermined Franco's claims to have created a free and independent Spain and his post-1945 policy of portraying a valiant Spain fighting alone against a hostile dangerous world.

The second was less immediate but in the long term more significant. The inevitable opening up of Spain to world finance also allowed other foreign influences to penetrate Spain's frontiers. The impact of television, films, books, magazines, of consumerism in general, of different political ideas and cultures, of tourists; all these would gradually take a hold on Spain's new generations as the memories of the Civil War slowly faded. Perhaps he recognised the mixed blessings of the US deal when he later sourly remarked that *the best thing the Americans did for us was to empty the Madrid bars and cabarets of whores, since they almost all marry American sergeants and GI's.*[87]

Franco's international rehabilitation was complete in December 1955 when the UN voted to allow Spain to joins its ranks. At home, meanwhile, Franco was beginning to devote ever more time to the pursuit of his many leisure activities. A regime newspaper described Franco at this time as the 'sentry of the West' and the 'Guardian of the European spiritual fortress' but the sentry was no longer always at his post. Instead Franco could be found deep-sea fishing, freshwater fishing, shooting, sailing or playing golf. Many of these passions he indulged in with businessman

Franco inspects a guard of honour aboard the American aircraft carrier Coral Sea. 1954

Max Borrell, one of the very few civilian friends the Generalísimo ever made. When Franco tired of these pastimes he spent time developing the large estate he had bought at Valdefuentes, near Madrid, or watching films in his private cinema at El Pardo. His favourite movies were westerns. Though Franco remained very much in control of affairs, and still chaired interminable Cabinet meetings, his day-to-day involvement in the details of Government was getting less and less.

Franco did manage to lose some weight, however, as during the decade he was put on a low calorie diet. This was not always successful, given his love of fattening dishes such as bean and sausage stew from Asurias (*fabada*) and the fact that supporters anxious to win his favour would give him tasty morsels during hunting trips. Franco's personal tastes were in most matters very simple. He never smoked, and rarely drank more than a glass of wine with a meal, followed perhaps by a post-dinner sherry or a coffee. Sometimes he would watch television – he loved football and boxing – or play cards with his old army cronies. He rose at around 7am and was generally a creature of habit in his work and leisure activities.

A constant in Franco's routine was the way he treated people and expected people to treat him. Not even Max Borrell, for example, was allowed to use the familiar 'tu' form of address in Spanish. Also, when meeting people Franco reportedly kept his right hand low by his side so that they had to bow slightly to shake his hand. Those who worked closely with him described his glacial behaviour towards colleagues and friends, even though to strangers he could be talkative and even appear amiable. His cousin and long-time aide Pacón noted how Franco was 'effusive with those who dominate him and with flatterers who swamp him with gifts and lavish hospitality, but as cold as an ice flow with the majority of us who are not sycophants...'. A minister and family friend José Antonio Girón claimed Franco exuded a 'coldness which at times freezes the soul'.[88] Franco seemed least open with people who knew him the best; this was possibly a form of defence mechanism. He also disliked telling ministers face to face that they had been sacked. Often they learnt of their dismissal by letter or even from reading the newspapers.

Carmen, too, could be a forbidding character. Like her husband, she had also learnt how to make the most of her position. For example, notoriously fond of money, she collected the many gold medals given to her husband by appreciative Spanish communities and had them melted down into ingots.

Franco and wife Carmen welcome the Shah of Iran and Queen on a State Visit to Madrid

Despite the successes of the early 1950s Franco was still bedevilled with the key questions of what the nature of the state was – and where was it heading. As the Civil War became more distant these questions became more pressing, and harder to answer. In October 1954 the role of the monarchy was highlighted once more with the coming of age of Don Juan's eldest daughter, known as the Infanta Pilar. Thousands of Spaniards joined the celebrations in Portugal, showing the enduring lure of the Bourbons. A number of monarchists meanwhile established a quasi-political movement known as the Third Force to lobby peacefully for a restoration.

Franco needed to regain control of the situation and once more met Don Juan, this time at a country estate in Extremadura, on 29 December 1954. Little of substance was agreed, though monarchists were heartened by Franco's apparent acceptance of the rights of the Bourbon dynasty. Franco had nevertheless temporarily managed to draw the sting out of the monarchist threat while making it clear he would never step down as head of state. What were most revealing were Franco's frank comments: On the one hand he boasted to Don Juan that Spain was *easy to govern* while on the other he showed a familiar self-pity when he complained that his work was not fully appreciated.[89]

If the monarchists were one part of the political problem, another was the Falangists. The regime's status as a monarchy – albeit without a king – caused disquiet among Falangists who feared that their long-awaited right-wing radical project had been permanently shelved. This was a view shared among impatient Falangist students. On 9 February 1956 Falangist students held a demonstration in Madrid to mark the death of a Falangist student martyr Matías Montero back in 1934. These students clashed with anti-Falangist counterparts and a Falange supporter Miguel Alvarez was shot and wounded. Though the shooting was almost certainly an accident, the incident quickly erupted into a major crisis as the Falangist press and activists called for bloody revenge. In response the military authorities, including senior generals General Agustín Muñoz Grandes and General Carlos Martínez Campos, warned they would not tolerate any attempt at revenge killings by Falangists.

In Spanish a respectful title for women similar to Madam is 'Doña' – hence Franco's wife was known as Doña Carmen. However, her love of jewellery earned her another name – 'Doña Collares' or 'Doña Necklaces'. She was equally fond of antiques too. Carmen had a reputation for using her name rather than money to acquire items. Antiques shops and jewellers would close when she was around to avoid having to donate items to her. It was even claimed that some Spanish jewellers set up a discreet insurance syndicate to protect themselves against the losses resulting from a visit.

Significantly, after being kept informed of events, Franco still chose to go on a hunting expedition. This was an early indication that he was slowly becoming distracted and starting to lose his usual grip on events. On 14 February, however, Franco, refreshed from his trip, sacked the education minister Joaquín Ruiz Giménez whose tentative reforms the Caudillo blamed for the unrest in the first place. To maintain his customary balance he also removed the head of the 'Movement' – as the FET y las JONS was known – Raimundo Fernández. The Caudillo then recalled his old Falangist crony Arrese to head up the FET.

Ten years after the end of the Second World War Franco may have described the Movement as little more than a *propaganda claque*, but he clearly still felt it had some useful functions.[90] He instructed Arrese to draw up new laws to institutionalise the regime. At the same time, and despite serious strikes in the north of the country, Franco and Arrese embarked on a tour of Andalusia at the end of April in which the Caudillo addressed tens of thousands apparently deliriously happy Spaniards. Franco had stepped back in time.

In the end Franco's nostalgic encouragement of the Falange and Arrese proved a political blunder. Arrese's proposals aimed to create a regime in which the Movement would be the dominant voice in government, at least once Franco was off the scene. The military, monarchists and senior Church hierarchy were united in their furious opposition to the plans. The ultra loyal and increasingly influential Carrero Blanco was also opposed. Eventually Franco was forced to back down and by the end of the year Arrese's radical proposals were, to his great disgust, shelved. The veteran Falangist complained that the country would once again be run by 'soldiers and priests'. However, the bitter reaction to Arrese's plans showed that Franco had gone too far in favouring one of the 'families' of the regime and had needed to retreat to prevent an even more grave political crisis. The Caudillo's pragmatic retreat tactics gave substance to the views of the British Ambassador Sir Ivo Mallet who considered Franco a 'complete cynic interested only in keeping power...' The diplomat repeated a story about how Franco had two folders on his desk, one marked 'problems which time will solve', the other 'problems which time has solved'. The Caudillo's favourite task, it was claimed, was to move files from one folder to the next.[91]

Yet the passage of time could nonetheless work against Franco. The other

Surrealist artist Salvador Dali in conversation with Franco at the El Pardo. 1956

big event of 1956 saw the end of one of his most cherished aims, a dream that had inspired him since his days as a young soldier. On 7 April 1956 Spain signed an agreement granting Spanish Morocco independence as part of a free Morocco.

Franco had grown up with the idea that a new empire in Africa was Spain's destiny, and he had personally fought for that goal. He had also had claimed that it was his years as a soldier in Africa that had defined him, while the idea of a building a new Spanish empire had also been a key plank of early Francoism. Yet now Franco had not only failed to extend Spain's empire but had impotently handed over most of what it already had. Though Morocco's independence was part of a wider international trend, the loss of Spain's African lands hit Franco hard.

Franco's renewed flirtation with the Falange in 1956 showed how the leader, who was now in his mid-60s, felt more comfortable with the old and the familiar. His realistic acceptance of the loss of Spanish Morocco meanwhile underline how in a changing world Franco was less and less able to control events. Increasingly the ageing leader would preside over a society he did not understand and try to steer Spain through an international landscape he did not recognise. After 1956 Franco would spend even more time on his pastimes and surround himself with a clique of people – among whom Carmen had a powerful voice – who shared his old-fashioned and prejudiced view of the world. Meanwhile a new generation of Spaniards would take over the day to day running of ever-more complex areas of government such as finance, trade and the economy in general.

As early as September 1945 Spain had been obliged to withdrawn her troops from Tangier, Franco's only imperial gain during the Second World War. From the early 1950's Franco had allowed anti-French nationalism to flourish in Spanish Morocco to discomfort France, without realising that this would create an unstoppable movement within the Spanish-held lands as well. When on 2 March the French announced independence for its Moroccan territories, the reaction in Spanish Morocco forced Franco to make a similar announcement on 15 March. Spain was left with its old colonies of Ceuta and Melilla, plus Ifni which was ceded to Morocco in 1969.

Franco's new Cabinet, announced on 22 February 1957, highlighted both these backward and forward-looking tendencies. The veteran soldier Muñoz Grandes – who had led the anti-Soviet Blue Division in the Second World War – was removed as Minister of War but given the title Captain General. Only monarchs and Franco had used this title before and it suggested that Muñoz Grandes was the man to take over from Franco if a crisis required it. The new Minister of the Interior, meanwhile, was General Camilo Alonso Vega, a friend since childhood days. At the same time Arrese was moved to Housing, a sign that the brief Falangist renaissance was definitively over.

Men such as Vega and Muñoz Grandes were Franco's political comfort blankets. The novelty of the new government, in which Carrero Blanco had a major hand, was the arrival of the so-called 'technocrats'. These were people who were less interested in politics per se and more interested in modern and efficient government. They included men such as Alberto Ullastres Calvo at Commerce and Mariano Navarro Rubio at Finance. Another crucial though less visible appointment was that of a brilliant young lawyer Laureano López Rodó as Carrero Blanco's number two. Like many of the technocrats he had close links with the Catholic organisation Opus Dei. The technocrats would have a huge influence on Spain over the next decade and a half, and be at least partly responsible for the economic boom that would help sustain Franco in power while simultaneously transforming Spanish society.

Franco later played down the importance of his new Cabinet, pointing out that it was a result of the need for new faces, wear and tear and *natural wastage*. Yet it was clear that Franco was partly leading, partly being dragged – by men such as Carrero Blanco and López Rodó – into a more modern form of government better suited to a complex world. There was a shift too in the way Franco was presented to the public. The balcony appearances, in which Franco came across as a remote leader, were reduced in number. Instead Franco became more visible, appeared at numerous opening ceremonies and was driven through towns to meet the public rather than talking down at them from balconies. Though he retained ultimate power, and would do for years to come, little by little Franco was becoming a figurehead in his own regime.[92]

The secular Catholic group Opus Dei – which means 'work of God' in Latin – was established in Madrid in 1928 by Josemaría Escrivá de Balaguer, who was made a saint after his death in 1975. As a priest Father Josemaría had fled from the widespread killing of clerics by Republicans during the Civil War. The controversial evangelical organisation has sometimes been accused of being secretive and manipulative, claims it strongly denies. In Spain technocrats such as López Rodó were members of Opus Dei and though relatively small in number the organisation's members had a significant impact on the Franco regime.

Franco himself was more and more wrapped up in his shooting and fishing. During one fishing trip to Galicia in 1958 he apparently caught a 20-ton whale. The following year he boasted of shooting nearly five thousand partridges in just a few day's hunting. Often he would fire more than five thousand cartridges in a single day. Franco's attitude to his sporting pursuits was revealing on a number of levels. His friend Max Borrell claimed that to watch Franco pursue a whale was to 'understand all the successes of his political and military careers…his perseverance is such that he would chase a whale to Russia.' Meanwhile Franco told Pacón how much he had revelled in the 20-hour struggle to catch the whale. *I really enjoy this sport and it is a great relief from my work and worries.*[93]

These worries included the proposal in February 1959 that Spain adopt a stabilisation plan in conjunction with the International Monetary Fund (IMF). This involved the devaluation of the peseta. Though the plan was deemed vital as the technocrats grappled with Spain's structural and economic problems, Franco refused to approve it, essentially on the basis that the IMF was run by untrustworthy foreigners. A deeply anxious Navarro Rubio sought a personal interview with the Caudillo to impress upon him the urgency of the situation. Eventually, after the finance minister raised the spectre of Spaniards once again having to use ration cards, Franco reluctantly relented. Though Franco was deeply suspicious of a financial world that increasingly baffled him, he was usually prepared to trust the judgement of expert ministers.

The leader was far more at home with his pet project at the Valley of the Fallen, which was a reassuring reminder of the past in an uncertain world. On 30 March 1959 the restless remains of the former Falange leader José Antonio Primo de Rivera were again dug up, this time from El Escorial, and re-buried in the valley's impressive Church of the Holy Cross. The next day, the 20th anniversary of the end of the Civil War, Franco and Carmen formally inaugurated the massive and costly monument which had taken nearly two decades to complete. In what was an almost mediaeval scene, the couple progressed slowly up the church aisle, Franco in the uniform of Captain General, Carmen all in black, towards their thrones near the altar. All the key figures of the regime were present, plus the diplomatic corps; workers were given a day's paid leave and a free lunch to enable

The sporting general and his trophies, a row of dead ducks

them to watch the ceremony. Surrounded by vivid memories of the past, Franco's speech emphasised the martial nature of the victory in 1939 and referred to those who had *had to bite the dust of defeat*. He had not preached reconciliation in April 1939, and he had no intention of doing so now.[94]

The decade ended on a high note for Franco as he proudly hosted a visit by the US President Dwight D. Eisenhower. When the American leader landed at Torrejón de Ardoz near Madrid, one of the US bases agreed under the 1953 pact, the Caudillo gushingly expressed his and Spain's *humble admiration* for him. Though initial relations between the pair were awkward, Eisenhower warmed to his companion when he discovered that Franco shared his love of partridge shooting. In the end the two men got on well, with Eisenhower even embracing the diminutive Franco as he left. The US president was struck by Franco's calm manners and later wrote: 'I was impressed by the fact that there was no discernible mannerism or characteristic that would lead an unknowing visitor to conclude that he was in the presence of a dictator.' Franco, meanwhile, barely suppressed his glee at his new friendship with the most powerful man in the world.[95]

Though the US president's visit was a boost for those looking to the future in Spain, Franco's preferred tendency was still to dwell in the past. His blinkered view of the world was perfectly illustrated months later in May 1960. In the first ever European Nations Cup the Spanish football team was drawn to play the Soviet Union in the two-legged quarter finals. At the time Spanish football was riding high, notably through the success of a Real Madrid side that had won the first European Cup final in 1956 and won the next four as well. Franco himself was a fan. Yet the Caudillo was warned that there might be pro-Soviet demonstrations at the game in Spain, and was also reminded that some combatants from the Blue Division still languished in Soviet concentration camps. He therefore insisted that both legs be played on neutral grounds. The Russians, well within their rights, refused and the matches were cancelled. Inevitably the tie was awarded to the Soviet team. Spanish football fans were massively disappointed but also baffled when their press initially failed to mention the incident at all. Instead they just noted that the Soviet team had made it to the semi-finals.

If Franco had managed to alienate Spanish football fans, he was also unpopular with certain members of his own political 'families'. Franco had always based his political success on careful balancing of the different groups who constituted Francoism. But he had recently downplayed the role of the Falange and the effects of this were shown graphically on 20

November 1960 when he attended a ceremony at the basilica at the Valley of the Fallen. As the lights dimmed a voice cried out: 'Franco, you are a traitor'. The person responsible, a young Falangist disillusioned with the inertia and corruption of the regime, was arrested. Though an affronted Franco initially wanted him shot, the youth was eventually sent instead to a punishment battalion in the Sahara Desert.[96]

Franco's lack of awareness of what was really happening in much of his own country was graphically shown in the spring of 1961 when on a tour of Andalusia a liberal-minded civil governor showed him the poverty of the shanty towns of Seville. Franco was genuinely shocked that such scenes existed in Spain. His solution, however, was not to adopt new policies but to appeal to the region's elite to lend a Christian hand to create *social justice*.[97]

As Franco approached his seventies, he continually had to face the question of what or who would follow his demise. On 29 March 1960 he had again met Don Juan, though the meeting decided little as by now Franco had privately made up his mind that in terms of a successor he would skip a generation to Don Juan's son Juan Carlos. However, he was careful not to say anything publicly for fear of alienating both father and son. However, the issue of who would succeed Franco was most forcibly rammed home after an incident on Christmas Eve 1961. While he was on a pigeon shoot, Franco's gun exploded and badly injured his left hand. For months the Caudillo would be in pain and discomfort from the wound. More important, however, was the sudden realisation among his supporters that their ageing leader, who had just celebrated 25 years as head of the Nationalist cause, was not, as some may have preferred to believe, immortal.

A Dying Regime 1964-1975

His shooting accident was not the Caudillo's only health problem during the 1960's. During the decade – though it was not publicised – Franco began to suffer from Parkinson's disease, a progressive neurological condition. This made him prone to shaking, affected his walking and on occasions caused his mouth to fall and remain open, lending him a vacant expression. The disease would come and go in its impact on Franco in the last 15 years of his life, but there was no disguising the slow physical decline he was suffering. This came as a shock to people in the regime, for Franco had enjoyed robust health for most of his life. Now his failing condition seemed to mirror a slow decay in Francoism itself.

Aside from his health, the 1960's brought problems Franco had not faced for more than two decades. After the brutal suppression of the Republican side in the Civil War and immediately afterwards, Franco's main opposition had come from within his own regime, something that he had skilfully managed by playing various factions off against another. Now there was a growing opposition in the rest of Spain too, from striking workers demanding better pay and conditions, from students, Basque and Catalan nationalists, and even some parts of the Catholic Church.

Franco showed his concern about the situation in June 1962. At the fourth congress of the European Movement in Munich – an organisation working for a united Europe – Spanish participants included dissident Falangists, liberal Catholics, exiled monarchists and democrats, socialists and Basque and Catalan nationalists. Franco was furious at this widespread and pubic display of opposition and on 8 June the 69-year-old chaired an all-night meeting of the Cabinet to decide how to react. The result was a virulent press campaign and the arrest of many of the participants. Meanwhile the Caudillo himself railed against *communist infiltration in*

Franco extends a warm welcome to King Hassan of Morocco. Madrid 1963

Europe and praised his own regime's *misunderstood* values. He insisted: *If we hold fast the barking out there from communism and its associates will matter little to us, since what matters is what goes on here at home.*[98]

What Franco seemed unable to grasp was that what happened at home could have a disastrous impact on Spain's reputation and potentially her economy. On 20 April 1963 a communist called Julián Grimau was shot by firing squad having earlier been arrested and tortured by Spanish security forces. Franco had typically refused to show any clemency, despite world-wide condemnation and appeals from religious leaders. The continuation of such repression in Spain was one reason why the country had no chance of joining the European Economic Community (EEC) as a full member, despite the hopes of the government's technocrats. Not that this worried Franco, as he saw the organisation as a hotbed of *liberals, Christian Democrats* and, worst of all, *freemasons.*[99] As ever, Franco was still fighting old and often imaginary battles of the past.

The celebrations of 1964, to mark 25 years of 'Franco's peace' since the end of the Civil War, were an attempt to marry Franco's obsession with the past with the more pressing task of demonstrating a continuing justification for the regime. Masterminded by the reform-minded Falangist minister Manuel Fraga Iribarne, they emphasized the material benefits that Franco had brought to Spain. One of the key planks of the year's events was the release of a film called *Franco, the man* (*Franco, ese hombre*) which portrayed him as the man who had not just saved his country from chaos and communism, but also given its people prosperity. Though many cinemagoers watched the film in Spain, Franco himself seemed not to enjoy it. At the end of the premiere at El Pardo, and within earshot of the director José Luis Sáenz de Heredia, the Caudillo drily commented that it contained *too many parades.*[100]

The years from 1961-1973 in Spain are sometimes called the 'years of development'. The economy grew on average at 7 per cent a year, one of the fastest rates in the world. By 1964 per capita income had reached $500 a year, which meant Spain was no longer classed by the UN as developing nation. It reached $1,239 by 1972. Part of the boom was caused by emigrant Spaniards sending money back home, but it was also fuelled by tourism. By 1964 the number of visitors had reached 14 million, and this rose to 34 million in 1973.[101]

Despite the comforting tones of the 1964 celebrations, and the swift if unevenly-distributed economic growth, the second half of the 1960's was to prove a troubling time for Franco and his regime. The Caudillo was in a classic dilemma. Spanish and world society was changing quickly, but the government itself was unsure of which way to move. The question for Franco and his supporters was whether, in order to maintain power, the regime needed slowly to reform to track those changes, or whether to retreat into the Francoist bunker. A third approach, espoused by many of the technocrats, held that economic prosperity alone was the key to survival. At various times in the late sixties and early seventies the regime ended up doing a bit of all three, partly reflecting the fact that Francoism was about survival rather than about pure ideology. It also reflected the fact that Franco, whose instincts were against any reform but who now lived in a world he barely understood, no longer had a sure feel for the best direction for the government. In 1966, for example, Franco reluctantly approved a new press law proposed by Fraga, but later complained that he was *fed up with the fact that the press wakes up each day asking itself what shall we criticise today.* He no longer felt master in his own country. Another insight into Franco's diminishing authority came when he told Carrero Blanco how he tried vainly to get rid of a minister whose policies he disliked. *I provoked him to make him offer [his resignation] but he didn't,* the Caudillo commented lamely.[102]

The greatest uncertainty that hung over the regime was the enduring question – and one that Franco was still very reluctant to face, at least publicly – about who or what came next. It was one issue guaranteed to make him bad tempered if it was ever raised at Cabinet. The government took a small step towards defining the nature of the regime in 1966 with the passing of the so-called Organic Law of the State *(Ley Orgánica del Estado).* Originally drafted by Franco himself, it defined Spain as a monarchy and also made provision for the position of a prime minister. On 22 November a frail Franco, who was now 73, presented the new legislation to the Cortes, taking the opportunity to denounce his critics and remind the nation he had saved Spain. The regime even held a referendum on the new law 14 December which suspiciously won more than 95 per cent approval out of the 88 per cent of eligible voters who supposedly took part.

Yet still the new law did not state who would take over once Franco was gone. The exasperation felt at this in many parts of the regime, including among many ministers and the royal family, was exemplified in January

King Juan Carlos and Queen Sophia of Spain seated with their children

1968 when Juan Carlos's son Felipe was born. At the christening Franco was confronted by Alfonso XIII's widow Queen Victoria Eugenia, the mother of Don Juan, grandmother of Juan Carlos and great-grandmother of the new baby. Indicating the different generations, the Queen said: 'Well Franco, you've got all three Bourbons in front of you. Decide!' The Caudillo, doubtless taken aback, gave no reply.[103]

However, Franco knew that soon he would have to decide – or rather make public his choice. For it seems clear that Franco had already decided that Juan Carlos would be his heir. He had discounted the Carlist pretender Carlos Hugo de Borbón partly on the grounds that he was too foreign, while Don Juan was altogether too liberal. The advantage of Juan Carlos was that he had been educated in the Spanish military under Franco's watchful eye and was already a semi-official figure within the regime. He was therefore more likely to provide continuity after Franco's death than any outsider.

Juan Carlos also showed that he had acquired some of Franco's cunning. On 8 January 1969, in remarks drafted by Fraga, the Prince made clear his support for the idea that the monarch should be 'installed' rather than 'restored'. For Franco this was a crucial distinction. It emphasised that the new monarchy would be a continuation of Francoism, rather than a return to Bourbon rule. A week later Franco made it clear to the prince that he would soon be named the heir. *Don't let yourself be influenced by anything else. Everything is prepared*, he told his protégé. The Prince replied: 'Don't worry *mi General*, I have already learned a great deal of your *galleguismo* (the cunning attributed to *gallegos*, natives of Galicia).'[104]

Juan Carlos, who was born in 1938 in Rome, was the son of Bourbon heir Don Juan. Educated in Spain, and in the Spanish military, both under the watchful eye of Franco, the tall young prince could appear awkward and reserved in public and was seen as someone Franco could manipulate. However, the astute Juan Carlos, who in 1962 married princess Sophia of Greece, came to realise that after Franco he would have to preside over a return to democracy. Even Franco refused to give him advice on government, accepting that Juan Carlos could never rule in the way he had.

In fact, and after being prodded yet again by Carrero Blanco to make a decision on the succession public, Franco showed he still had some of his own guile left. When Juan Carlos went off in the early summer to visit his father Don Juan, Franco deliberately withheld from him the fact that he was shortly to make an announcement. Franco later told the prince that this was so that if Don Juan asked about the succession, Juan Carlos would not be obliged to lie to his father. In reality the Caudillo did it to drive a wedge between the father and son. Franco told the Cabinet on 21 July of his decision and announced it the following day in the Cortes. On 23 July Juan Carlos swore loyalty to the Head of State and the principles of the Movement, while in exile his surprised and dismayed father Don Juan dissociated himself from the whole proceedings. Nearly 30 years after the end of the Civil War, Franco finally had his heir as head of state.

Though the issue of the succession had taken up a good deal of Franco's time, he was more and more pre-occupied with less taxing matters. Tired, and perhaps frustrated by affairs of state, Franco's already lengthy holidays became longer and he continued to shoot and fish despite his declining health. He had also taken up more sedentary pursuits and like many men of his age in Spain had taken to doing the football pools. Indeed in May 1967 Franco won one million pesetas – about £6,000 at the time.

Though he still oversaw the regular Friday Cabinet meetings his frailty was shown when for the first time in December 1968 and again in January 1969, the Caudillo had to leave the meeting to answer a call of nature. Ever since his leadership in the Civil war his staff had boasted how Franco could work for a whole day without leaving his desk. This was a small but telling sign that the Caudillo's legendary powers were waning.

A more potent sign that the regime itself was in decay was a huge financial scandal that broke publicly less than a month after Juan Carlos had sworn his oath of allegiance. The saga involved a Pamplona-based textile company known as MATESA, which had received billions of pesetas in export credits from the government after inflating its orders. The company simply claimed it had been acting with the knowledge of officials to get around rigid bureaucracy. However, for the Falangist and its press this was a long-awaited chance to attack the influence of the Opus Dei technocrats, some of whom were heavily implicated in the affair.

Franco, who had always taken a relaxed attitude towards allegations of financial as opposed to sexual misconduct, did not personally view the allegations too seriously. He defended Opus Dei ministers and officials as *perfect gentlemen*. Franco also bluntly told leading Falangists he believed their main grudge against Opus Dei members was that *while they work you just fuck about.*[105]

Yet the magnitude of the scandal demanded action. On 29 October 1969, guided by Carrero Blanco, Franco held one of the biggest Cabinet reshuffles of his life, bringing in thirteen new members. Two ministers linked to the scandal were dropped, but so too were the Falangist José Solís Ruiz who was accused of stirring up reaction against Opus Dei, and the minister of press and information Fraga. Carrero personally blamed Fraga for a liberalisation of media and general censorship that had – so he believed – allowed pornography, strip tease, Marxist and anarchist literature, immoral theatre and a general air of negativity into Spanish society. The make up of the new cabinet was in fact more technocrat and pro-Opus Dei than ever. However the real winner was Carrero Blanco. Though he turned down Franco's suggestion that he become Prime Minister, it was Carrero Blanco who was the main driving force of the government. Juan Carlos may have been the heir as head of state, but the true heir of Francoism was the Admiral who had loyally served his master for more than 30 years.

Franco's harsh treatment of the Basques, notably at Guernica in 1937 but also afterwards, had ensured deep resentment of the regime among many of its people. In 1960's the letters ETA were first seen – standing for Euskadi Ta Askatasuna or 'Basque Homeland and Freedom'. A section of ETA advocated violence to achieve its nationalist ends and the first act of terrorism took place in 1961. ETA members and other Basque nationalist who were arrested by the security forces were often brutally tortured. The organisation's biggest blow against Franco was the murder of Prime Minister Carrero Blanco in 1973.

The MATESA scandal brought huge discredit to the regime, at home and abroad, despite attempts by Franco to bring an end to it by offering a pardon to those involved in October 1971. By then Franco's government had also been under fire for its reaction to yet another major threat, this time from Basque nationalism.

On 18 September 1970 the cause of Basque nationalism was brought to worldwide attention at the Jai alai Championships in San Sebastián – jai alai (or pelota as it is also called) is a sport similar to squash. A Basque veteran of Guernica in 1937 set himself alight and badly burnt himself in front of an apparently unperturbed Franco, who carried on watching the game. The visit of President Nixon soon afterwards offered Franco a brief respite from the issue of the Basques. But in December the trial of ETA militants in Burgos attracted yet more international coverage, as well raising the political temperature in Spain itself. Three ETA members were sentenced to death. Eventually, and against his own inclination, Franco agreed with Carrero Blanco that it would be a blunder to allow the executions to take place and the ageing Caudillo commuted the sentences to life imprisonment.

The damage, however, was already done. On the one hand Franco had alienated much of international opinion as well as many Catholics and moderates at home. On the other the so-called 'bunker' of people who surrounded him – and they included the ultra-conservative Carmen – felt that the technocrats were weak and pandering to the opposition. Spain and the regime were becoming increasingly polarised.

As for Franco himself, he was increasingly detached from reality. On 1 October 1971 he addressed a large crowd from the balcony of the Palacio de Oriente in Madrid to mark thirty-five years as head of the nationalist cause. As he looked down on the sea of blue-shirted Falangists chanting his name in front of him, the 78-year-old could have been forgiven for thinking that the ordinary people of Spain passionately supported him. In fact it was a stage-managed event of die-hard supporters, who themselves knew that without Franco they had no chance of any influence in Spain.

The extent to which not just Franco but also Carmen was losing a grip on the real world was shown in the build up to the wedding on 18 March 1972 of their eldest granddaughter Maria del Carmen to Alfonso de Borbón Dampierre. Alfonso was the eldest son of Don Jaime, the son of the late Alfonso XIII who as a deaf mute had renounced his claim to the throne, which passed to Don Juan (though Don Jaime later tried to retract his renunciation). Before the wedding – at which the Filipino dictator's wife Imelda Marcos was a guest – Carmen launched a campaign to have Alfonso officially recognised as 'His Royal Highness' and a full royal prince effectively on a par with his first cousin Juan Carlos. Carmen also insisted that servants should address her granddaughter as 'Your Highness'. The suspicion was that Carmen hoped to change the succession so that her own flesh and blood could one day help form a Franco dynasty. Some in the close-knit and ultra-right 'bunker' favoured such a move over the succession of Juan Carlos whom they and Carmen felt was dangerously liberal. Franco liked the idea of his granddaughter being a princess but showed no inclination to change his plans for the succession and Carmen's scheming eventually came to nothing.

The signs of decay, dissatisfaction and unrest in the regime were now unmistakable. Franco's older brother Nicolás was implicated in a major olive oil financial scandal in the spring of 1972, while on 3 April police killed a striker near Barcelona. Strikes and violence were becoming increasingly commonplace, and even the Church openly distanced itself from Francoism. Then on 1 May members of a far-left organisation known as FRAP hacked to death a policeman in Madrid. The ultra right took this as a sign that the regime should return to tough repressive measures and even martial law. Meanwhile Carmen had already spoken darkly of the 'disloyalty' of the Minister of Interior Tomás Garicano Goñi, who himself resigned on 7 May in alarm at the growing activity of the 'ultra' right.[106]

Franco finally persuaded a still reluctant Carrero Blanco to become prime minister to steady the ship of state. The fearful Franco also insisted that the hard-line Carlos Arias Navarro, a favourite of his wife, be made Minister of Interior. Carmen's influence seemed to grow as Franco's diminished. This reactionary government had little time to act, however. For at 9.25am on 20 December 1973 Carrero was assassinated by a bomb as he drove to work after attending Mass. The ETA assassins had dug a tunnel under a street that Carrero Blanco used each day and had let off the explosives as his car passed overhead. The force of the explosion threw the vehicle onto the fourth floor roof of a nearby church.

Franco was devastated by the loss of a man who had been his utterly loyal servant for decades. Carrero Blanco, who had no threatening personal ambition of his own, had shared the same aims and the same prejudices as his master. If anyone could have inherited the mantle of Francoism it was Carrero Blanco. But now he was gone. The next day Franco wept at a brief Cabinet meeting. Later he said of Carrero Blanco's death: *They have cut my last link with the world.* Meanwhile one minister Gonzalo Fernández de la Mora commented: 'No harder blow could have been struck at the future prospects of the state of 18 July (i.e. Franco's regime.)[107]

The 'bunker' around Franco grew in influence after Carrero Blanco's death. It included figures such as José Antonio Girón de Velasco and Franco's son-in-law the Marqués de Villaverde, as well as Carmen herself. It was she who is said to have helped Franco to choose Arias Navarro as the new premier over other candidates with the words: 'They are going to kill us all like Carrero Blanco. We need a hard president. It has to be Arias.'[108] In the end Arias produced a mixture of reform and reaction that was to please neither the reform-minded nor the ultra right. The bunker's anxiety was further increased in April 1974 the Portuguese dictatorship fell after 45 years, an omen of what could happen in neighbouring Spain.

Franco, who had stubbornly insisted on continuing to shoot, had been suffering from leg pains and fungal infections of the mouth, and the effects of Parkinson's disease were now very apparent. On 9 July he had to be treated by his doctor Vicente Gil for a blood clot, caused so the doctor thought by Franco sitting through every televised match of the football World Cup. On 18 July his condition worsened and the following day Juan Carlos took over as temporary Head of State as provided for in the constitution. However, Franco rallied and on 2 September resumed his position as Head of State once more, incidentally without informing Juan Carlos first.

During the winter of 1974/1975 the increasingly senile and frail Franco went on a number of hunting trips despite the inclement weather. In May 1975 meanwhile he opened the May Fair and received the visit of President Gerald Ford. It was as if, fearful of the time after Franco, elements of the regime – and the bunker especially – wanted to persuade themselves that

In his final years, Franco photographed at his desk. 1973

life was carrying on as normal in Spain. They were not, however, as Franco was fading quickly. Even now, though, the old man's resolute opposition to opening up Spain to the scourge of democracy was still apparent. When he read a modest proposal by former minister Fraga for a political association, a still lucid Franco asked bitingly *for what country is Fraga writing these projects?*[109] The habitual contempt for international opinion was also shown by the Caudillo's approval in September 1975 of the death sentence for convicted members of FRAP, despite a wave of appeals and condemnation from abroad.

The end came soon, though not swiftly or painlessly. In the middle of October he suffered a mild heart attack, after which he continued to work until another attack on 20 October. The frail old man was also hit by recurring dental problems, stomach complaints and by the end of the month peritonitis. On 30 October he handed over power, this time permanently, to Juan Carlos. By 5 November Franco was in hospital in Madrid and he needed three operations to stop internal bleedings. Kept alive for two weeks, apparently at the behest of a fearful 'bunker', it was his daughter Nenuca who finally persuaded doctors to let her father die in peace. At 5.25am on 20 November 1975 Francisco Bahamonde Franco was officially declared dead.

Franco's political will, which was read out to the nation at 10am, showed a small degree of contrition. *I beg forgiveness of everyone, just as with all my heart I forgive those who declared themselves my enemies even though I never thought of them as such,* he wrote. *I believe that I had no enemies other than the enemies of Spain.* Franco reminded the Spanish people, however, that his fight was still necessary even though he was in his grave. *Do not forget that the enemies of Spain and of Christian civilization are on the alert.*[110]

General Franco had brought the Spanish people 35 years of stability, relative peace and ultimately some prosperity, though it had been at a terrible cost. He did not though leave a lasting political legacy. Within a relatively short time of the Caudillo's slow and painful death his successor as Head of State King Juan Carlos was presiding over a liberal democratic monarchy of the kind that Franco had long and loudly despised. Interestingly, the number of votes cast for the left and right in elections in 1977 was almost the same as those cast in February 1936. A newspaper carried this news under the desolate headline 'Forty Wasted Years'.[111]

In the end, Francoism, which died with Franco, had been about staying in power while maintaining a view of the world that had been formed by the first half of the 1930's. A fellow Africanista, Colonel Segismundo Casado, had once summed up Franco's simple approach to ruling Spain. Casado believed that Franco typified the mentality of the Spanish foreign legionnaire. 'We are told "Take so many men, occupy such-and-such a position and do not move from there until you get further orders" . The position occupied by Franco is the nation and since he has no superior officer, he will not move from there.'[112] In the end, only death could make him do that.

Endnotes

[1] Quoted at Paul Preston, *Franco: A Biography* (HarperCollins, London: 1993) p 29.

[2] Francisco Franco, *Palabras del Caudillo 19 Abril 1937 – 31 Diciembre 1938* (Ediciones Fe, Barcelona: 1939) p 314.

[3] Preston, *Franco* p 29

[4] Interview with Carmen Polo, *Estampa*, 29 May 1928.

[5] Preston, *Franco* p 30

[6] *El Carbayón*, 22 February 1922

[7] Quoted at Preston, *Franco* p 466

[8] Gabrielle Ashford Hodges, *Franco: A Concise Biography* (Weidenfeld & Nicolson, London: 2000), p 53.

[9] J. Arrarás, *Franco* (Librería International, San Sebastian: 1937) pp 158-159

[10] R. Garriga, *Ramón Franco, el hermano maldito* (Editorial Planeta, Barcelona: 1978) pp 209–210

[11] Sheelagh Ellwood, *Franco: Profiles in Power* (Longman, London: 1994) p 38

[12] F. Franco *"Apuntes" pesonales del Generalísimo sobre la República y la guerra civil* (Fundación Nacional Francisco Franco, Madrid: 1987) p5

[13] Ashford Hodges, *Franco*, p 67

[14] J. Arrarás, Franco (Librería International, San Sebastian: 1937) pp 159 – 160

[15] 'Discurso de despedida en el cierre de la Academia General Militar', *Revista de Historia Militar*, Año XX, No 40, 1976 pp 335 – 7

[16] F. Franco *"Apuntes" pesonales del Generalísimo sobre la República y la guerra civil* (Fundación Nacional Francisco Franco, Madrid: 1987) p 4

[17] R. Baón, *La cara humana de un caudillo* (Editorial San Martín, Madrid: 1975) p 110

[18] C. Martín, *Franco, soldado y estadista* (Fermín Uriarte, Madrid: 1965) pp 129–130

[119] Comments to Italian *Chargé d'Affaires* Geisser Celesia, quoted Preston, *Franco* p 106

[20] F. Franco *"Apuntes" pesonales del Generalísimo sobre la República y la guerra civil* (Fundación Nacional Francisco Franco, Madrid: 1987) p 13

[21] Preston, *Franco* p 106

[22] F. Franco Salgado-Araujo, *Mi vida junto a Franco* (Editorial Planeta, Barcelona: 1977) p 122.

[23] F. Franco *"Apuntes" pesonales del Generalísimo sobre la República y la guerra civil* (Fundación Nacional Francisco Franco, Madrid: 1987) p 18.

[24] Antony Beevor, *The Spanish Civil War* (Cassell Military Paperbacks, London 1999) p 31

[25] J. Arrarás, *Franco* (Librería International, San Sebastian: 1937) p 198

[26] G. Hills, *Franco, The Man and His Nation* (Robert Hale, London: 1967) pp 209–210

[27] Preston, *Franco* pp 117–118

[28] F. Franco *"Apuntes" pesonales del Generalísimo sobre la República y la*

guerra civil (Fundación Nacional Francisco Franco, Madrid: 1987) p 33

29 Preston, *Franco* p 121

30 Preston, *Franco* p 134

31 Preston, *Franco* pp 126-127

32 I Prieto, *Palabras al viento* (Mexico City: 1969) p 221

33 J. Arrarás, *Franco* (Librería International, San Sebastian: 1937) pp 240-244. See also Preston, *Franco* pp 131-133 and Sheelagh Ellwood, *Franco: Profiles in Power* (Longman, London: 1994) pp 65-66 for a discussion of the letter.

34 *The Morning Post*, 20 July 1937, quoted in Preston, *Franco* p 137

35 Preston, *Franco* p 140

36 J. Arrarás, *Franco* (Librería International, San Sebastian: 1937) pp 263-271.

37 Preston, *Franco* p 473

38 *The News Chronicle*, 1 August 1936. Quoted Preston, *Franco* p 153

39 Antony Beevor, *The Spanish Civil War* (Cassell Military Paperbacks, London 1999) pp 103–104

40 Preston, *Franco* p 181. For a discussion of Franco's tactics see Beevor, *The Spanish Civil War* pp 102–103

41 Preston, *Franco* p 183

42 Preston, *Franco* p 184

43 Preston, *Franco* p 186

44 John Whitaker, *Prelude to World War: A Witness from Spain* (Foreign Affairs, Vol 21, no 1: October 1942) p 115. quoted at Preston, *Franco* p 204

45 Preston, *Franco* p 212

46 Ellwood, *Franco* pp 95-96

47 Preston, *Franco* p 254

48 Ashford Hodges, *Franco*, pp 123-124

49 Ashford Hodges, *Franco* p 128

50 Foreign office papers, quoted at Preston, *Franco* p 298; Payne, *Regime* pp 194-195.

51 Preston, *Franco* p 305

52 Ciano, Diary 1937-1938 p 148 Quoted at Preston, *Franco* p 312

53 Preston, *Franco* p 312-313

54 Quoted at Preston, *Franco* p 315. See also. Payne, *Regime* pp 195-196

55 Franco, Francisco, *Palabras del Caudillo 19 Abril 1937 – 31 Diciembre 1938* (Ediciones Fe, Barcelona: 1939) p 209

56 Ellwood, *Franco* p 106

57 Payne, *Regime* pp 223-224. For a full discussion of the death toll see Payne, chapter 12. The study referred to was carried by Ramón Salas Larrazábal, *Pérdidas de la guerra,* (Barcelona: 1977)

58 Preston, *Franco* p 323

59 Preston, Franco p 317. For a discussion of Franco's gifts see Mariano Sánchez Soler, Villaverde: fortuna y caída de la casa Franco (Barcelona: 1990).

60 Preston, Franco p 196

61 Preston, Franco pp 351-352.

62 Juan Pablo Fusi, Franco: A Biography (Unwin Hyman London: 1987) p 41

63 Sir Samuel Hoare, Viscount

Templewood, Ambassador on Special Mission (Collins, London: 1946) pp 45-48, quoted at Ashford Hodges, Franco pp 164-165

[64] Preston, Franco pp 356-357

[65] Quoted at Preston, Franco p 386

[66] Preston, Franco pp 368-370; Ashford Hodges, Franco p 168; Payne Regime p 269

[67] Fusi, *Franco*, pp 51-52; Payne, *Regime* p 273; Preston, *Franco* pp 394-400

[68] Preston, *Franco* pp 397-398

[69] Ashford Hodges, *Franco* p 17.

[70] Ellwood, *Franco* pp 127-128

[71] Preston, *Franco* pp 430-431

[72] Ellwood, *Franco* pp 130-132; Fusi, *Franco* pp 52-53

[73] Payne, *Regime* pp 282-283

[74] See Preston, *Franco* pp 455-456; Ashford Hodges, *Franco* pp 184-185

[75] Payne, *Regime* pp 306-311; Preston, *Franco* pp 466-469

[76] See Stanley G. Payne *The Franco Regime* 1936-1975 (Phoenix Press, London: 2000) p 309; Paul Preston, *Franco: A Biography* (HarperCollins, London: 1993) p 465.

[77] Fusi, *Franco* p 49; Ashford Hodges, *Franco* p 196

[78] Gerald Brenan, *The Face of Spain* (Penguin, London: 1965) pp 48-49

[79] Ashford Hodges, *Franco* p 204; Preston, *Franco* pp 536-537

[80] Payne, *Regime* p 349; Ashford Hodges, *Franco* p 205

[81] Ellwood, *Franco* p 144; Preston, *Franco* pp 555-556

[82] *Arriba*, 10 December 1946

[83] F. Franco, *Discursos y Mensajes del Jefe del Estado , 1951-1954* (Dirección General de Información Publicaciones Españolas, Madrid: 1955) pp 7–20

[84] Fusi, *Franco* pp 70–72

[85] Quoted at Preston, *Franco* p 612

[86] F. Franco, *Discursos y Mensajes del Jefe del Estado , 1951-1954* (Dirección General de Información Publicaciones Españolas, Madrid: 1955) p 401. See also Payne, *Regime* p 349, pp 420-421

[87] Ashford Hodges, *Franco* pp 218-219

[88] Preston, *Franco* pp 628-629

[89] Preston, *Franco* pp 637–638; Fusi, *Franco* pp 81-82

[90] Payne, *Regime* p 444

[91] Preston, *Franco* p 648

[92] Fusi, *Franco* pp 94-95

[93] Ashford Hodges, *Franco* p 231

[94] Preston, *Franco* p 679

[95] Preston, *Franco* p 680-681

[96] Preston, *Franco* p 697

[97] Preston, *Franco* p 691

[98] F. Franco, *Discursos y Mensajes del Jefe del Estado , 1960-1963* (Dirección General de Información Publicaciones Españolas, Madrid: 1964) pp 399-404; see also Ellwood, *Franco* p 196-197

[99] Preston, *Franco* p 700

[100] Ellwood, *Franco* p 199

[101] John Hooper, *The Spaniards: A Portrait of New Spain* (Penguin, London: 1987) pp 26-29; Fusi,

Franco pp 110-112.
[102] Preston, *Franco* p 728; pp 724-725.
[103] Preston, *Franco* pp 735-736
[104] Payne, *Regime* p 541
[105] Preston, *Franco* pp744-745
[106] Payne, *Regime* pp 585-586
[107] Preston, *Franco* p 762; Fusi, *Franco* p 148
[108] Preston, *Franco* p 764
[109] Preston, *Franco* p 774
[110] *Arriba*, 25 November 1975, quoted at Preston, *Franco* p 779
[111] John Hooper, *The Spaniards: A Portratit of New Spain* (Penguin, London: 1987) pp 33-34
[112] Quoted at Preston, *Franco* p 184

Further Reading

Ashford Hodges, Gabrielle, *Franco: A Concise Biography* (Weidenfield & Nicolson, London: 2000): an interesting biography that pays special attention to the complex psychology of Franco.

Beevor, Antony, *The Spanish Civil War* (Orbis, London: 1982): a readable and vivid account of the civil war.

Brenan, Gerald, *The Spanish Labyrinth: An Account of the Social and Political Background of the Spanish Civil War* (Cambridge University Press, Cambridge: 1990): one of the classic studies of the build up to the civil war.

Brenan, Gerald, *The Face of Spain* (Penguin, London: 1965): eyewitness accounts of Franco's regime after the Second World War.

Carr, Raymond, *Spain: A History* (OUP, Oxford: 2000): authoritative, concise history of Spain edited by the doyen of Spanish history.

De Blaye, Edouard, *Franco and the Politics of Spain* (Pelican, London: 1976): originally written in the last years of the Franco regime.

Ellwood, Sheelagh *Franco: Profiles in Power* (Longman, London: 1994): thoughtful and very readable examination of Franco and his politics.

Fletcher, Richard, *Moorish Spain* (Phoenix, London: 1994): an intelligent look at Moors in Spain and their influence on Spanish history and culture.

Fusi, Juan Pablo, *Franco: A Biography* (Unwin Hyman London: 1987): a balanced biographical essay by a Spanish author, with a preface by Raymond Carr.

Hooper, John, *The Spaniards: A Portrait of New Spain* (Penguin, London: 1987): a guide to the way Spain has changed in comparison with the days under Franco.

Kamen, Henry, *The Spanish Inquisition: An Historical Revision* (Phoenix, London: 1998): a new look at one of the most interesting and important parts of Spanish history.

MacKay, Angus, *Spain in the Middle Ages: From Frontier to Empire,*

1000–1500 (Macmillan, London: 1977): charts the shaping of Spanish society during and after the Reconquest.

Orwell, *George Homage to Catalonia* (Penguin, London: 1989): compelling description of the author's time fighting for the Republican cause in the Spanish Civil war.

Payne, Stanley G, *The Franco Regime* 1936-1975 (Phoenix Press, London: 2000): scholarly examination of Franco's rise to power and his government from a leading authority.

Pendle, George, *A History of Latin America* (Penguin, London: 1963): concise study that also charts the end of Spain's vast empire in the Americas.

Preston, Paul, *A Concise History of the Spanish Civil War* (Fontana Press, London: 1996): an authoritative account of the civil war.

Preston, Paul, *Franco: A Biography* (HarperCollins, London: 1993): a comprehensive, detailed, scholarly and very readable account of Franco's life that is probably the definitive study in any language.

Thomas, Hugh, *The Spanish Civil War* (Penguin, London: 2003): A revised edition of the 1961 classic account of the civil war.

Picture sources

Year	Age	Life
1892		4 December; Francisco Franco Bahamonde born at El Ferrol, Galicia, to parents Nicolás and Pilar.
1905	12	Enters Naval Preparatory School, El Ferrol.
1907	14	29 August the teenager enters the Military Academy in Toledo. Father Nicolás moves to a post in Madrid and effectively ends his unhappy marriage to Pilar.
1910	17	In June, completes military studies. 13 July is commissioned as Second Lieutenant, placed 251st out of 312 cadets in his year. 23 July posted to 8th Infantry Regiment, El Ferrol
1912	19	February, posted to Morocco. 13 June, promoted to first lieutenant.
1913	20	Joins native police, the Regulares. 12 October awarded Military Merit Cross, first class.
1915	22	Promoted to Captain, effective from 1 February 1914.
1916	23	29 June, seriously wounded in stomach during attack on El Biutz.
1917	24	2 February, promoted to major, with effect from 29 June 1916. 1 March, posted to Oviedo, Spain. August, takes part of repression of strike in Asturias. Meets Carmen Polo

Year	History	Culture
1892	Panama scandal breaks in France: Ferdinand de Lesseps accused of corruption	Claude Monet begins pictures of Rouen Cathedral (- 1895)
1905	"Bloody Sunday" in St Petersburg. German Emperor's visit to Tangiers sets off "First Moroccan Crisis".	Louis Vauxcelles coins the name *Les Fauves* for group of artists around Matisse. Debussy, *La Mer*. Shaw, *Major Barbara*.
1907	Anglo-Russian Entente. Electric washing-machine invented.	The Saturday Evening Post reports that daily attendance at nickelodeons exceeds 2 million.
1910	death of King Edward VII; succeeded by George V. Portugal proclaimed a republic.	Ralph Vaughan William, *A Sea Symphony*. E M Forster, *Howard's End*
1912	Titanic sinks. Dr Sun Yat-sen establishes Republic of China. Stainless steel invented.	Arnold Schoenberg, *Pierrot lunaire*. Carl Jung, *The Psychology of the Unconscious*. Bertrand Russell, *The Problems of Philosophy*.
1913	In US, Woodrow Wilson becomes president (until 1921). Hans Geiger invents Geiger counter.	Stravinsky, *The Rite of Spring*. Guillaume Apollinaire, *Les peintres cubistes*. D H Lawrence, *Sons and Lovers*. Marcel Proust, *A la recherche du temps perdu* (until 1927).
1915	Dardanelles/Gallipoli campaign (until 1916). Italy denounces its Triple Alliance with Germany and Austria-Hungary.	Twelve-reel *Birth of a Nation,* first modern motion picture, grosses $18m. Picasso, *Harlequin*.
1916	23	
1917	In Russia, Tsar Nicholas II abdicates: Communists seize power under Vladimir Lenin. US enters First World War. Balfour Declaration on Palestine: Britain favours creation of Jewish state without prejudice to non-Jewish communities.	First recording of New Orleans jazz. Franz Kafka, *Metamorphosis*. T S Eliot, *Prufrock and Other Observations*. Giurgio de Chirico, *Le Grand Métaphysique*.

Year	Age	Life
1920	27	October, returns to Africa as second-in-command of new Spanish Foreign Legion.
1922	29	Writes of his exploits in Africa under title Morocco: The Diary of a Battalion.
1923	30	June, promoted to lieutenant colonel, takes over command of Spanish Foreign Legion. 22 October, marries Carmen Polo.
1925	32	February, promoted to Colonel, with effect from January 1924. Takes part in landing at Alhucemas.
1926	33	3 February, promoted to brigadier general. Leaves Africa and joins prestigious First Brigade of First Division in Madrid. 14 September, birth of only child, Carmen.
1928	35	Becomes director of Military Academy, Zaragoza. Visits German Infantry Academy, Dresden.
1931	38	Left without posting after Academy closes under new Republican government. Farewell speech to cadets.
1932	39	February, appointed to command 15ths Infantry Brigade, Corunna.
1933	40	Appointed General Commander, Balearic Islands.

Year	History	Culture
1920	IRA formed. First meeting of League of Nations	June: Provides score for *George White's Scandals of 1920*
1922	Soviet Union formed. Benito Mussolini's fascists march on Rome.	
1923	Ottoman empire ends; Palestine, Transjordan and Iraq to Britain; Syria to France.	Le Corbusier, *Vers une architecture*
1925	Pact of Locarno, multilateral treaty intended to guarantee peace in Europe. Chiang Kai-shek launches campaign to unify China. Discovery of ionosphere.	Erik Satie dies. F Scott Fitzgerald, *The Great Gatsby*. Kafka, *The Trial*. Sergey Eisenstein, *Battleship Potemkin*. Television invented.
1926	Germany joins League of Nations. Hirohito becomes emperor of Japan.	Hemingway, *The Sun Also Rises*. A A Milne, *Winnie the Pooh*. Fritz Lang, *Metropolis*
1928	Kellogg-Briand Pact for Peace. Transjordan becomes self-governing under the British mandate. Albania is proclaimed a kingdom. Alexander Fleming discovers penicillin.	Maurice Ravel, *Boléro*. Kurt Weill, *The Threepenny Opera*. Huxley, *Point Counter Point*. D H Lawrence, *Lady Chatterley's Lover*. W B Yeats, *The Tower*. Walt Disney, *Steamboat Willie*.
1931	New Zealand becomes independent. Japan occupies Manchuria. Building of Empire State Building completed in New York.	Antoine de St-Exupéry, *Vol de nuit/Night Flight*. Rakhmaninov's music is banned in Soviet Union as 'decadent'. Chaplin, *City Lights*.
1932	Kingdom of Saudi Arabia independent. Kingdom of Iraq independent. James Chadwick discovers neutron. First autobahn opened, between Cologne and Bonn.	Aldous Huxley, *Brave New World*. Jules Romains, *Les homes de bonne volonté*. Bertolt Brecht, *The Mother*. Thomas Beecham founds London Philharmonic Orchestra.
1933	Adolf Hitler appointed German chancellor. F D Roosevelt president in US; launches New Deal.	André Malraux, *La condition humaine*. Gertrude Stein, *The Autobiography of Alice B Toklas*.

Year	Age	Life
1934	41	28 February, mother dies. Meets father for last time at reading of will. Promoted to Major-General, returns to Madrid as adviser to Minister of War. October, heads suppression of revolutionary strike in Asturias.
1935	42	February, appointed Commander-in-Chief of Armed Forces in Spanish Morocco. 17 May, appointed Chief of General Staff in Madrid.
1936	43	28 January, represents Republic at funeral of King George V at Westminster Abbey. 17 February, after victory of Popular Front in elections, tries but fails to get martial law declared across Spain. Removed as Chief of General Staff but appointed General Commander of Canary Islands. 8 March, attends meeting of senior army officers to discuss possible coup. 11 March arrives in Canary Islands. 23 June writes letter to Prime Minister Casares Quiroga hinting he should be put in full charge of armed forces. 12 July, tells fellow conspirators he will not join coup. 13 July, after murder of right wing leader José Calvo Sotelo, tells conspirators he will join coup. 18 July flies to Morocco as head of army revolt in Africa as Civil War begins. 19 July seeks help from Mussolini to get army across to Spain. 3 August, becomes member of National Defence Council, main body of the Nationalist rebellion. 1 October, voted by fellow generals, becomes Head of State of Nationalist Spain and Generalissimo of Armed Forces. November, fails to take Madrid.
1937	44	19 April, announces formation of new unified state party, the 'Movement'. Denies responsibility for bombing of Guernica on 26 April.
1938	45	30 January, names first cabinet, with influential brother-in-law Ramón Serrano Suñer as Minister of Interior. March, launches new Labour Charter. 29 October, learns of death of younger brother Ramón in air crash.
1939	46	1 April, Franco's HQ announces end of Civil War. 19 May, salutes massive victory parade in Madrid. 9 August announces new Cabinet 4 September, declares Spain's neutrality in European war. 18 October Moves HQ to Madrid.

Year	History	Culture
1934	In China, Mao Zedong starts on the Long March. Enrico Fermi sets off first controlled nuclear reaction.	Shostakovich, *The Lady Macbeth of Mtsensk*. Agatha Christie, *Murder on the Orient Express.* Henry Miller, *Tropic of Cancer*
1935	42	
1936	Germany occupies Rhineland. Edward VIII abdicates throne in Britain; George VI becomes king. Spanish Civil War (until 1939).	RCA experiments with television broadcasts from the Empire State Building.
1937	Japan invades China: Nanjing massacre. Arab-Jewish conflict in Palestine.	Jean-Paul Sartre, *La Nausée.* John Steinbeck, *Of Mice and Men.* Picasso, *Guernica*
1938	Kristallnacht: in Germany, Jewish houses, synagogues and schools are burnt down, and shops looted. Austrian Anschluss with Germany.	Warner Brothers produce *Confessions of a Nazi Spy,* although Germany represents 30% of the profits.
1939	1 September: Germany invades Poland. Britain and France declare war on Germany.	Steinbeck, *The Grapes of Wrath.* John Ford, *Stagecoach* (starring John Wayne). David O Selznick, *Gone with the Wind* (starring Vivien Leigh and Clark Gable)

Year	Age	Life
1940	47	March, moves into new home, Royal hunting lodge El Pardo. 12 June, alters Spain's status to 'non-belligerence'. 14 June Franco orders troops to occupy tangier. 16 October appoints Serrano Suñer as Foreign Minister. 23 October, meets Hitler at Hendaye.
1941	48	12 February, meets Mussolini at Bordighera. 13 February, meets Pétain at Montpellier. June, authorises Blue Division of right-wing volunteers to fight with Germans on Soviet front. 8 December, congratulates Japan on Pearl Harbour attack.
1942	49	23 February, father dies. 3 September, sacks Serrano Suñer.
1943	50	17 March, opens first session of Cortes. September, agrees to withdraw Blue Division 1 October, returns Spain's official status to neutrality.
1944	51	October, asks Churchill to agree to Anglo-Spanish alliance against Bolshevism. 31 October, recognises provisional government in France.
1945	52	17 July, puts forward Spaniards' Charter. 18 July, names prominent Catholic politician Alberto Martín Artajo as Foreign Minister.
1947	54	June, hosts visit of Eva Perón – Evita. Wins national referendum on Law of Succession.
1948	55	25 August, meets Don Juan de Borbón on board yacht *Azor*.

Year	History	Culture
1940	Germany occupies France, Belgium, the Netherlands, Norway and Denmark. In Britain, Winston Churchill becomes PM. Leon Trotsky assassinated in Mexico.	Graham Greene, *The Power and the Glory.* Ernest Hemingway, *For Whom the Bell Tolls.* Chaplin, *The Great Dictator.* Disney, *Fantasia.*
1941	Operation Barbarossa: Germany invades Soviet Union. In US, Lend-Lease Bill passed. Churchill and F D Roosevelt sign Atlantic Charter. Japan attacks Pearl Harbour: US enter Second World War. In US, Manhattan Project begins.	First commercial television station begins broadcasting. Fitzgerald's Hollywood novel, *The Last Tycoon*, is published posthumously.
1942	Battle of El Alamein. US General MacArthur appointed C-i-C, Far East.	A. Camus, *L'Etranger.*
1943	Allies bomb Germany. Allies invade Italy: Mussolini deposed. Albert Hoffman discovers hallucinogenic properties of LSD.	Rodgers and Hammerstein, *Oklahoma.* Sartre, *Being and Nothingness.* T S Eliot, *Four Quartets*
1944	Allies land in Normandy: Paris is liberated. Civil war in Greece.	*Lay My Burden Down* (documentary about former slaves). Adorno and Horkheimer's essay on the 'Culture Industry'
1945	8 May: 'V E Day'. General election in Britain brings Labour landslide. 14 August: Japan surrenders, end of World War II.	B. Britten, *Peter Grimes.* G. Orwell, *Animal Farm.* K. Popper, *The Open Society and Its Enemies.*
1947	Truman Doctrine: US promises economic and military aid to countries threatened by Soviet expansion plans. India becomes independent. Chuck Yeager breaks the sounds barrier.	Tennessee Williams, *A Streetcar named Desire.* Albert Camus, *The Plague.* Anne Frank, *The Diary of Anne Frank.*
1948	Marshall plan (until 1951). Soviet blockade of Western sectors of Berlin: US and Britain organize	Brecht, *The Caucasian Chalk Circle.* Greene, *The Heart of the Matter.* Norman Mailer, *The*

Year	Age	Life
1949	56	22 October, state visit to Portugal.
1950	57	10 April, hosts wedding of daughter Nenuca to Dr Cristóbal Martínez Bordiu, the Marqués de Villaverde, at chapel at El Pardo.
1951	58	18 July, names fifth government, and appoints the influential Luis Carrero Blanco as Cabinet Secretary.
1953	60	27 August, signs Concordat with Vatican. 26 September, signs defence agreement, the Pact of Madrid, between US and Spain.
1954	61	9 December, birth of first grandson Francisco. 29 December, meets Don Juan in Extremadura.
1956	63	7 April, forced to accept independence of Morocco and the effective end of any Spanish empire in Africa.
1957	64	27 February, forms sixth government including the so-called 'technocrats' of the Catholic lay organisation Opus Dei.
1958	65	17 May, unveils the Fundamental Principles of the Movimiento in the Cortes.

Year	History	Culture
	airlift. In South Africa, Apartheid legislation passed. Gandhi is assassinated. State of Israel founded.	*Naked and the Dead.* Alan Paton, *Cry, the Beloved Country.* Vittorio De Sica, *Bicycle Thieves*
1949	NATO formed. Republic of Ireland formed. Mao proclaims China a People's Republic.	George Orwell, *1984.* Simone de Beauvoir, *The Second Sex.* Arthur Miller, *Death of a Salesman.*
1950	Schuman Plan. Korean War begins. China conquers Tibet. Stereophonic sound invented. First successful kidney transplant.	In US, McCarthyism starts (to 1954). Billy Wilder, *Sunset Boulevard.*
1951	Anzus pact in Pacific.	J D Salinger, *The Catcher in the Rye*
1953	Stalin dies. Mau Mau rebellion in Kenya. Eisenhower becomes US president. Korean War ends. Francis Crick and James Watson discover double helix (DNA).	Dylan Thomas, *Under Milk Wood.* Arthur Miller, *The Crucible.* Federico Fellini, *I Vitelloni.*
1954	Insurrection in Algeria. French withdrawal from Indochina: Ho Chi Minh forms government in North Vietnam.	Kingsley Amis, *Lucky Jim.* J R R Tolkien, *The Lord of the Rings.* Bill Haley and the Comets, *'Rock Around the Clock'*
1956	Nikita Khruschev denounces Stalin. Suez Crisis. Revolts in Poland and Hungary. Fidel Castro and Ernesto 'Che' Guevara land in Cuba. Transatlantic telephone service links US to UK.	Lerner (lyrics) and Loewe (music), *My Fair Lady.* Elvis Presley, *'Heartbreak Hotel'*, *'Hound Dog'*, *'Love Me Tender'.* John Osborne, *Look Back in Anger.*
1957	Treaty of Rome: EEC formed. USSR launches Sputnik 1. Ghana becomes independent.	The Academy excludes anyone on the Hollywood blacklist from consideration for Oscars (to 1959).
1958	Fifth French Republic; Charles De Gaulle becomes president. Great Leap Forward launched in China (until 1960). Castro leads communist revolution in Cuba.	Boris Pasternak, *Dr Zhivago.* Claude Lévi-Strauss, *Structural Anthropology.* Harold Pinter, *The Birthday Party.*

Year	Age	Life
1959	66	1 April, inaugurates Valley of the Fallen. December, plays host to President Eisenhower.
1961	68	24 December, injured in shooting accident.
1962	69	10 July, names sixth government, appoints veteran General Augustín Muñoz Grandes as Vice-President of the Council of Ministers and Manuel Fraga Iribarne as the new Minister for Information.
1963	70	April, approves execution of communist Julián Grimau.
1964	71	Celebrates 'twenty-five years of peace'.
1966	73	14 December, wins national referendum on Organic Law of the State.
1967	74	21 September, appoints Carrero Blanco as Vice-President of the Council of Ministers.
1969	76	January-March, orders state of emergency over student unrest. 22 July, officially names Don Juan's son Juan Carlos as his successor. 29 October, names ninth government.

Year	History	Culture
1959	In US, Alaska and Hawaii are admitted to the union. Solomon Bandaranaike, PM of Ceylon (Sri Lanka), is assassinated.	In Detroit, Berry Gordy founds Motown Records. Buddy Holly dies in plane crash. *Ben Hur* (dir. William Wyler). Günter Grass, *The Tin Drum*
1961	Berlin Wall erected. Bay of Pigs invasion. Yuri Gagarin is first man in space.	The Rolling Stones are formed. Rudolf Nureyev defects from USSR.
1962	Cuban missile crisis. Jamaica, Trinidad and Tobago, and Uganda become independent. Satellite television launched.	Edward Albee, *Who's Afraid of Virginia Woolf?* David Lean, *Lawrence of Arabia*
1963	J F Kennedy assassinated; Martin Luther King leads March on Washington. Kenya becomes independent. Organisation of African Unity formed.	Betty Friedan, *The Feminine Mystique*. The Beatles, 'She Loves You'. *Cleopatra* (Richard Burton and Elizabeth Taylor).Luchino Visconti, *The Leopard*.
1964	Khruschev ousted by Leonid Brezhnev. First race relations act in Britain. Civil Rights Act in US. PLO formed. Word processor invented.	Harnick (lyrics) and Bock (music) *Fiddler on the Roof*. Saul Bellow, *Herzog*. Stanley Kubrick, *Doctor Strangelove*
1966	France withdraws its troops from NATO. In the US, race riots. Smith declares Rhodesia a republic.	John Lennon speculates that the The Beatles are more popular than Jesus. The band gives their last concert.
1967	Six day War between Israel on the one side and Syria and Egypt on the other. First heart transplant.	The Beatles, *Sergeant Pepper's Lonely Hearts Club Band*. Gabriel García Márquez, *One Hundred Years of Solitude*. Tom Stoppard, *Rosencrantz and Guildenstern are Dead*.
1969	Neil Armstrong takes first moon walk. Internet created by US Department of Defence. Massive anti-war rallies in US.	Mario Puzo, *The Godfather*. *Easy Rider* (Dennis Hopper and Peter Fonda). *Midnight Cowboy* becomes first wide-released X-rated film.

Year	Age	Life
1970	77	October, hosts visit of President Nixon. December, commutes deaths penalties of ETA militants sentenced to death at trial in Burgos to life sentences.
1972	79	18 March, sees eldest granddaughter Carmen marry Alfonso de Borbón-Dampierre.
1973	80	8 June, appoints Carrero Blanco as Prime Minister. 22 October, celebrates golden wedding anniversary. 20 December, Carrero Blanco killed by ETA bomb. 29 December, names Carlos Arias Navarro as new Prime Minister.
1974	81	11 July, illness forces absence from Cabinet meeting for only second time. 14 July, hands over to Juan Carlos as interim Head of State 2 September, resumes as Head of State.
1975	82	May, hosts visit by President Ford. 26 September, approves execution of five people convicted of terrorism charges. 15 October, suffers minor heart attack 20 November, dies, aged 82.

Year	History	Culture
1970	First-ever meeting of East and West German heads of government. In Cambodia: Prince Sihanouk is overthrown, US troops withdraw and Khmer Rouge takes over.	Simon and Garfunkel, *Bridge Over Troubled Water.* The Beatles officially split up. Death from drug overdose of guitarist Jimi Hendrix.
1972	In US, Watergate scandal. Bloody Sunday massacre (N Ireland). Allende overthrown in Chile; Pinochet takes power. World Trade Centre completed. Optical fibre is invented.	Richard Adams, *Watership Down.* Bertolucci, *Last Tango in Paris.* Francis Ford Coppola, *The Godfather*
1973	Yom Kippur War. Denmark, Ireland and Britain enter EC. US withdraws from Vietnam War. OPEC oil crisis.	Pink Floyd, *The Dark Side of the Moon.* Larkin, *High Windows.* E F Schumacher, *Small is Beautiful.* Truffaut, *Day for Night*
1974	Watergate scandal; US President Richard Nixon forced to resign. Cyprus invaded by Turkey. Haile Selassie deposed in Ethiopia.	Dario Fo, *Can't Pay? Won't Pay!* Solzhenitsyn is expelled from the Soviet Union.
1975	Franco dies; King Juan Carlos restored in Spain. Angola and Mozambique become independent. End of Vietnam War. Khmer Rouge seize power in Cambodia. Civil War in Lebanon. Apollo and Soyuz dock in space.	Boulez, *Rituel in memoriam Bruno Maderna.* Queen, 'Bohemian Rhapsody'; first major rock video. Steven Spielberg, *Jaws.*

INDEX

abortion, 69
Africa, 62; Franco's career in,
 5, 10–14, 16, 26, 37, 40–1,
 44, 54, 73, 78, 115; Spanish
 interests in, 6, 8, 77, 81, 115;
 Franco arrives to lead coup, 30,
 35, 38–40; German interest in,
 78
Africanistas, 9, 12–14, 16, 22–3,
 25, 28, 60, 85, 135
Agadir, 38
Agustina , 89
Alcalá Zamora, Niceto, 27, 29, 31
Alfonso XIII, King, 8, 12, 17, 52;
 steps down, 20, 21; relatives, 45,
 87, 126, 130; death, 86
Alhucemas, 13
Alicante, 75
Alonso Vega, General Camilo, 5,
 116
Alvarez, Miguel, 113
Andalusia, 28, 41, 114, 121
Annual, 11–12
anti-clericalism, 70, 117
anti-Semitism, 81
Arburúa, Manuel, 105
Arias Navarro, Carlos, 132
Army of Africa, 27, 37–41, 43, 50
Arrese, José Luis de, 87, 114, 116
Assault Guards, 35
Asturias, 9, 39, 56; revolt, 25–7,
 29, 33, 41

Attlee, Clement, 95
Azaña, Manuel, 22–4, 27, 29;
 prime minister, 30–1, 34; flees
 to France, 64

Badajoz, 41
Bahamonde y Pardo de Andrade,
 Pilar, 1–2, 4–5, 23, 69, 89;
 Catholicism, 2, 9, 67; death, 24
Balearic Islands, 24
Balmes, General Amado, 37
baraka, 8
Barcelona, 1, 6, 39, 131; falls
 to Nationalists, 60, 63;
 demonstrations over Gibraltar,
 104
Barroso, Major Antonio, 30
Basque country, 20, 39, 55–6;
 identity suppressed, 70, 71;
 nationalism, 122, 129
Bebb, Captain William Henry, 38
Beigbeder, Juan, 85
Berbers, 5, 11
Berlin, 40, 62, 64
Bilbao, 56
Black Shirts, 51, 66
Blue Division, 89, 116, 120
Bolín, Luis, 35, 40
Borbón Dampierre, Alfonso de,
 130–1
Bordighera, 85
Borrell, Max, 109, 111, 118
Bourbon dynasty, 112–13, 126–7
braceros, 28
Brenan, Gerald, 96, 102
Britain, 21; and Spanish Civil
 War, 51, 62, 64; during Second

World War, 79, 80–2, 88–9, 91; condemns Franco regime, 97; and Gibraltar, 104
Brunete, 59
Burgos, 39, 42, 59, 60, 73, 130

Cabanellas, General Miguel, 40, 45, 48
Cáceres, 48
Cadiz, 4, 33
Calvo Sotelo, José, 35
Canada, 82
Canary Islands, 31, 33, 35, 80, 97
Carlists, 52–4, 59, 66, 71, 90, 127
Carmen Polo y Martínez Valdés, María del: Franco meets, 9–10; Catholicism, 9, 22, 67, 107; marriage, 12–13, 91, 104; influence on Franco, 13, 55; gives birth to daughter, 15; and military coup, 33, 38, 42; lives like queen at El Pardo, 73–4, 78, 87; acquisitiveness, 73, 111, 113; at pro-Franco demonstration, 98; and Eva Perón, 99–100; importance of social status, 102, 113; increasing influence, 13, 116, 130–2; inaugurates Valley of the Fallen monument, 118; and succession, 130–1
Carmen Polo y Martínez Valdés, Zita, 55, 91
Carrero Blanco, Luis, 87; influence as minister, 105, 114, 116, 125, 127, 129–30; assassinated, 129, 131–2

Casablanca, 35, 38
Casado, Colonel Segismundo, 135
Casares Quiroga, Santiago, 34, 42
Castejón, Major Antonio, 50
Castilblanco, 23
Catalonia, 20, 25; fall of, 60, 63–4; identity suppressed, 70, 71; nationalism, 122
Catholic Church, 6, 20, 67, 97, 107, 114; opposition to Franco, 122, 131
Catholicism, 2, 4, 9, 20, 43, 53, 71, 107
CEDA, 26, 27, 29, 31, 33, 53–4
Ceuta, 5, 8, 116
Churchill, Winston, 92, 95, 98, 106
Civil Guard, 20, 23–4, 39, 42
Cold War, 101, 106
Comintern, 29–30
communism, 20–1, 28, 52, 70, 94–5, 98, 124; Franco's denunciations of, 25, 31, 87–9, 99, 105, 122
Condor Legion, 55–6
Córdoba, 96
Cuba, 3, 77
Cuelgamuros, 75
Cuenca, 33
Czechoslovakia, 62

divorce, 68
dolphin sandwiches, 85, 87
Don Carlos, 52, 127
Don Jaime, 130
Don Juan, 27, 52, 86, 126–8, 130; banished from Spain, 45; life,

87; issues 'manifesto', 92–4; moves to Portugal, 97; ruled out of succession, 99–101, 121, 127; meets Franco, 100–1, 112–13, 121

Ebro, battle of, 61–2
Eisenhower, Dwight D, 119–20
El Biutz, 8
El Cid, 67
El Escorial, 75, 118
El Ferrol, 1–5, 15
El Pardo, 73, 78, 87, 102, 106, 110, 124
Escrivá de Balaguer, Josemaria, 117
Estoril, 97
ETA, 129, 130–1
European Economic Community (EEC), 124
Extremadura, 28, 41, 43, 112

Falange, 33, 53–4, 59, 71, 87, 96; role in post-war regime, 98–9, 113–15, 120, 128
fascism, 51, 52; semi-fascism, 71
Felipe, Prince, 126
Fernández de la Mora, Gonzalo, 132
Fernández, Raimundo, 114
FET y de las JONS, 54, 70, 73, 87, 114
First World War, 8
football, 120, 128, 132
Ford, Gerald, 132
Fraga Iribarne, Manuel, 124–5, 127, 129, 133
France, 5, 21, 89; and Spanish

Civil War, 51, 60, 62, 64; Vichy, 80, 82; condemns Franco regime, 97; and Moroccan independence, 116
Franco, Carmen ('Nenuca'), 33, 38, 42, 59, 87; birth, 15; marriage, 102–4
Franco Bahamonde, Francisco: birth, 1; personality, 2, 4–5, 59; coldness and detachment, 2, 24, 57, 59, 62–3, 111; physical appearance, 2, 4, 40, 57, 59, 73, 78, 95, 111; early military career, 2–13; wounded in stomach, 8, 9; sexuality, 9; brutality, 11, 25–6; commands Foreign Legion, 12–14; marriage, 12–13, 91, 104; commands First Brigade, 14; prudence, 14, 30; political skills, 14, 23, 35, 54, 62, 71, 87; Director of Military Academy, 15–19, 21–2; ignorance of strategy, 16; reputation for discipline, 17; Catholicism, 20, 22, 45, 53, 67, 107; anti-communism, 20–1, 70, 87–9, 95, 101, 105, 122; antipathy to freemasonry, 21, 96, 105–6, 124; commands brigade in La Coruña, 23; General Commander of the Balearic Islands, 24; and mother's death, 24; suppresses Asturias revolt, 25–6, 27, 33, 41; sense of mission to save Spain, 25, 31, 36, 41, 42; Commander-in-

Chief of Army of Africa, 27;
Chief of Central General Staff,
27–31; General Commander
of the Canary Islands, 31–7;
passion for golf, 33; learns
English, 33; intends to stand for
election, 33–4; joins coup, 35–
9; emerges as Nationalist leader,
40–5; emerges as Generalísimo,
45–6; becomes head of state, 45,
48, 50; cult of personality, 48,
98; superstition, 52; consolidates
leadership, 52–5, 56–7; and
bombing of Guernica, 55–6;
love of titles and awards, 60,
81; love of comfort, 63;
love of triumphalism and
pageantry, 65–7, 75–6, 91, 102;
institutionalises power, 72, 114;
semi-regal style, 72–4; pastimes,
73, 78, 98, 109–11, 113, 116,
117–18, 120, 128, 132; salary,
73; commissions Valley of the
Fallen monument, 75, 118;
complacency, 78; responses to
Second World War, 80–94;
meets Hitler, 81–5; gullibility,
85; writes novel, 85–6, 102;
importance of social status,
86, 102; 'two wars' theory, 88;
and father's death, 89; self-pity,
98, 113; receives international
visitors, 99–100, 107–9, 119–
20, 130, 132; meets Don Juan,
100–1, 112–13, 121; as father
and grandfather, 102, 104, 130;
personal tastes, 111; cynicism,

114; becomes a figurehead, 117;
sustains injury, 121; suffering
from Parkinson's disease, 122,
132; death and political will,
134–5
Franco Bahamonde, Nicolás, 1, 3,
63; adviser to Franco, 42, 45,
55; inherits father's baton, 89;
implicated in financial scandal,
104, 131
Franco Bahamonde, Paz, 1
Franco Bahamonde, Pilar, 1, 2, 5
Franco Bahamonde, Ramón, 1, 15,
21; threatens coup, 18, 20, 39;
death, 62–3
Franco Salgado-Araujo, Nicolás,
1–2, 24; affairs, 1, 4, 9, 69;
Franco's last meeting with, 25;
death, 89
Franco the man (*Franco ese hombre*),
124
Francoism, 13, 90, 115; nature
of, 120, 125; decay of, 122;
continuation of, 127, 129,
131–2; death of, 134
FRAP, 131, 134
freemasonry, 21, 45, 79, 96, 101,
105–6, 124

Galarza, Colonel Valentín, 87, 90
Galicia, 1, 4, 39, 63, 117
gallegos, 14, 71, 127
García, Cristino, 97
Garicano Goñi, Tomás, 131
George V, King, 30
Germany, 42, 51, 53–4, 62, 71,
96; war aims, 75–7, 82; invades

Soviet Union, 87–90
Gibraltar, 81, 82, 104
Gil, Vicente, 132
Gil Robles, José, 26–9
Girón de Velasco, José Antonio, 111, 132
Goebbels, Josef, 13
Gomá, Cardinal, 67
Gómez Jordana, General Francisco, 91
Gran Canaria, 36–7
Griffis, Stanton, 102
Grimau, Julián, 123
Guadalajara, 52
Guernica, 55–6, 129, 130

Hedilla, Manuel, 54
Hendaye, 81
Hidalgo, Diego, 25
Hitler, Adolf, 40, 48, 90, 94, 106, 108; and Spanish Civil War, 51, 62; relationship with Franco, 75, 77–85, 96
Hoare, Sir Samuel, 78, 81
Hodgson, Sir Robert, 59, 62

Ifni, 116
Infanta Pilar, 112
International Brigades, 51, 52
International Monetary Fund, 118
International Red Cross, 70
Italy, 42, 51, 53–4, 71, 75, 87, 96

Jaca, 19, 22
jai alai (pelota), 130
Japan, 89, 94
Jarama, 52

Juan Carlos, King, 87, 101, 126–9, 131; succession, 101, 127; takes over as head of state, 132, 134

Kindalán, General Alfredo, 42, 45, 48, 97

La Coruña, 23, 63
Largo Caballero, Francisco, 31, 34, 42, 50
Las Palmas, 37–8
Latin America, 3
Lausanne, 93
Law of Responsibilities, 63
Law of Succession, 99
Le Havre, 38
League of Nations, 106
Lennard, Dora, 35
Lerroux, Alejandro, 24, 29
London, 30, 40
López Rodó, Laureano, 117

Madrid, 1, 4, 14, 17, 24–5, 31; air raid on royal palace, 20; churches burned, 22; political violence, 35; stays loyal to Republic, 39; Nationalists attack, 42, 44, 49–50; fall of, 64; victory parade, 65–7; Franco takes up residence, 73; pro-Franco demonstration, 98; Falangist rallies, 113, 130; policeman murdered, 131
Málaga, 52
Mallet, Sir Ivo, 114
Mallorca, 62–3
Maria Christina, Queen, 17

Marshall Aid, 96
Martí, José, 3
Martín Artajo, Alberto, 97
Martínez Campos, General Carlos, 113
MATESA scandal, 128–9
Melilla, 5, 6, 11, 13, 116
Mexico, 94
Millán Astray, Major José, 9–12, 42, 45
Mola Vidal, General Emilio, 28; leads coup plot, 31–2, 34–6, 40, 42; life, 39; conduct of war, 45; response to Franco as head of state, 48; leads attack on Madrid, 49; death, 56
Montero, Matías, 113
Morocco, 5, 12, 14, 35, 40, 77, 80; Franco in, 6, 13, 25, 27–8; gains independence, 115–16
Moscardo, Colonel, 43
Munich, 122
Muñoz Grandes, General Agustín, 113, 116
Mussolini, Benito, 40, 48, 94, 106; and Spanish Civil War, 51, 62; relationship with Franco, 75, 77–8, 85, 96

NATO, 104
Navarre, 39
Navarro Rubio, Mariano, 117–18
Negrín, Juan, 64
Nixon, Richard M, 130
North Africa, 80, 82, 91

Opus Dei, 117, 128–9

Organic Law of the State, 125
Orwell, George, 52
Oviedo, 9, 12, 22

Pacón, 3, 5, 22, 33, 38, 111, 118
Pamplona, 36
Paris, 17, 30
penal labour, 65
Perón, Eva, 99–100
Perón, Juan, 99
Pétain, Marshal Henri, 80
Philip, Duke of Wharton, 106
Philippines, 3
Picasso, Pablo, 56
Pius XII, Pope, 67, 107
Pollard, Hugh, 35–6
Popular Front, 29–30
Portela, Manuel, 30
Portugal, 81, 97, 112; dictatorship falls, 132
Prieto, Indalecio, 31, 34
Primo de Rivera, General Miguel, 12, 14–17, 72
Primo de Rivera, José Antonio, 33–4, 53; exhumation and reburial, 75, 118
Puerto Rico, 3
Pyrenees, 93

Queipo de Llano, General Gonzalo, 21, 38, 40, 45

Real Madrid, 120
Regulares, 7, 25
Ribbentrop, Joachim von, 80
Rif, 5
Rojo, General Vicente, 49, 58, 64

Rome, 40, 62, 64
Roosevelt, Franklin D, 106
Ruiz Giménez, Joaquín, 114
Russia, 51

Sáenz de Heredia, José Luis, 124
Sahara Desert, 121
St Teresa of Avila, 52
Salamanca, 39, 45, 48, 55
San Sebastian, 21
Sanjurjo, General José, 20, 23–4, 27, 31, 35, 40, 42
Santa Cruz, 36
Santander, 56
Santoña, 56
Scotland, 33
Second World War, 77, 79, 95, 116
Segovia, 39
Segura, Cardinal Pedro, 107
Serrano Súñer, Ramón, 59, 73, 75, 80, 85, 89; life, 55; sacked as adviser, 90–1
Seville, 22, 40–1, 107, 121
Solís Ruiz, José, 129
Sophia of Greece, Princess, 127
Soviet Union, 106, 120; aid for Republicans, 49, 51; German invasion, 87–90
Spain: empire, 3, 77, 80; involvement in Africa, 6, 14; under Primo de Rivera, 12, 14–17; Second Republic, 20–4, 28, 34–5, 38–9, 45, 48, 63–4, 67, 70; First Republic, 21; general strike, 25; Moorish invasion and *Reconquista*, 26, 55, 70; land ownership, 28–9,

70; public view of Franco, 34; military coup, 37–50, 52; Civil War, 51–64, 67, 80, 98; gold reserves, 51; neutrality, 62, 78–9, 82, 85, 91–3; Civil War casualties, 65; nature of Franco regime, 67–70, 95–7, 107, 125; economy, 77, 95–6, 102, 104–5, 109, 117–18, 123–5; secret protocol with Germany, 84; attempted invasion, 93; press and censorship, 94, 101, 103, 105, 109, 120, 122, 125, 129; international attitudes towards, 94, 96, 98, 101–2, 109, 134; Vatican Concordat, 107–8; US bases, 109, 120; influence of technocrats, 116–18, 124–5, 128–30; growing opposition to Franco, 122; returns to democracy, 127, 133–4; influence of 'bunker' around Franco, 130–2
Spaniards' Charter, 97
Spanish-American War, 3
Spanish Army, 4, 11, 21, 60; split by coup, 39; shattered by Civil War, 77; *see also* Army of Africa
Spanish Foreign Legion, 9–14, 25, 47
Spanish Inquisition, 70
Spanish Military Union (UME), 28
Spanish Navy, 2–3, 39, 60
Spanish Socialist Workers' Party (PSOE), 31
Stalin, Josef, 51, 89, 95, 97
Stalingrad, battle of, 90

Straits of Gibraltar, 40–1
Suanzes, Juan Antonio, 105
Sudetenland, 62

Talavera, 43
Tangier, 77, 79, 116
Tarragona, 63
television, 109, 111
Tenerife, 36–7
Teruel, 59
Tetuán, 8, 38, 40
Third Force, 112
Toledo, 3, 4, 6, 11; relief of Alcázar,
    42–5, 48
Torréjon de Ardoz, 120
Truman Harry S, 95, 106

Ullastres Calvo, Alberto, 117
United Nations, 94, 98, 101, 106,
    109, 124
United States of America, 3, 21;
    wartime relations with Spain,
    81, 89, 91; condemns Franco
    regime, 97; change in attitude to
    Spain, 101–2, 108–9

Valdefuentes, 110
Valencia, 39, 62, 65; government
    in, 50, 58
Valley of the Fallen, 75, 118, 121
Varela, General Enrique, 43, 90
Victoria, Queen, 17
Victoria Eugenia of Battenberg,
    Queen, 17, 126
Villaverde, Cristóbal Martínez
    Bordiú, Marqués de, 102–4,
    132

Viñuelas, 73

Waddell, Alexander, 81
Whitaker, John, 50
wolfram, 78, 91

Yague, Colonel Juan, 5, 25, 41, 60;
    adviser to Franco, 42, 45, 47, 85

Zaragoza, 15, 17, 19, 22; rising
    in, 40

LIFE & TIMES FROM HAUS

Alexander the Great
by Nigel Cawthorne
'moves through the career at a brisk,
dependable canter in his pocket
biography for Haus.'
BOYD TONKIN, The Independent
ISBN 1-904341-56-X (pb) £9.99

Armstrong
by David Bradbury
'it is a fine and well-researched
introduction'
GEORGE MELLY Daily Mail
ISBN 1-904341-46-2 (pb) £8.99

Bach
by Martin Geck
'The production values of the book
are exquisite.' Guardian
ISBN 1-904341-16-0 (pb) £8.99
ISBN 1-904341-35-7 (hb) £12.99

Beethoven
by Martin Geck
'...this little gem is a truly handy
reference.' Musical Opinion
ISBN 1-904341-00-4 (pb) £8.99
ISBN 1-904341-03-9 (hb) £12.99

Bette Davis
by Laura Moser
'The author compellingly unearths
the complex, self-destructive woman
that lay beneath the steely persona
of one of the best-loved actresses of
all time.'
ISBN 1-904341-48-9 (pb) £9.99

Bevan
by Clare Beckett
and Francis Beckett
"Haus, the enterprising new
imprint, adds another name to its
list of short biographies ... a timely
contribution.'
GREG NEALE, BBC History
ISBN 1-904341-63-2 (pb) £9.99

Brahms
by Hans A Neunzig
'These handy volumes fill a gap in
the market for readable,
comprehensive and attractively
priced biographies admirably.'
JULIAN HAYLOCK, Classic fm
ISBN 1-904341-17-9 (pb) £8.99

Caravaggio
by Patrick Hunt
'a first-class, succinct but comprehensive,
introduction to the artist'
BRIAN TOVEY The Art Newspaper
ISBN 1-904341-73-X (pb) £9.99
ISBN 1-904341-74-8 (hb) £12.99

Churchill
by Sebastian Haffner
'one of the most brilliant things of
any length written about Churchill'
TLS
ISBN 1-904341-07-1 (pb) £9.99
ISBN 1-904341-49-7 (CD) £12.95
ISBN 1-904341-43-8 (AC) £12.95

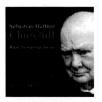

Curie
by Sarah Dry
'... this book could hardly be bettered'
New Scientist
selected as
Outstanding Academic Title by Choice
ISBN 1-904341-29-2 (pb) £8.99

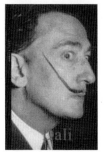

Dali
by Linde Salber
'a fascinating view on this flamboyant
artist, the central and most excentric figure
in Surrealism, seen through the prism
of psychological analysis'
ISBN 1-904341-75-6 (pb) £9.99

De Gaulle
by Julian Jackson
'this concise and distinguished book'
Sunday Telegraph
ISBN 1-904341-44-6 (pb) £9.99

Dostoevsky
by Richard Freeborn
'wonderful ... a learned guide'
JOHN CAREY The Sunday Times
ISBN 1-904341-27-6 (pb) £8.99

Dvořák
by Kurt Honolka
'This book seems really excellent to me.'
SIR CHARLES MACKERRAS
ISBN 1-904341-52-7 (pb) £9.99

Einstein
by Peter D Smith
'Concise, complete, well-produced and
lively throughout, ... a bargain at the
price.' New Scientist
ISBN 1-904341-14-4 (hb) £12.99
ISBN 1-904341-15-2 (pb) £8.99

Gershwin
by Ruth Leon
'Musical theatre aficionados will relish
Ruth Leon's GERSHWIN, a succinct
but substantial account of the great composer's
life'
MICHAEL ARDITTI, The Independent
ISBN 1-904341-23-3 (pb) £9.99

Johnson
by Timothy Wilson Smith
'from a prize-winning author a biography
of the famous and perennially fascinating
figure, Samuel Johnson'
ISBN 1-904341-81-0 (pb) £9.99

Joyce
by Ian Pindar
'I enjoyed the book very much, and
much approve of this skilful kind of popularisation.
It reads wonderfully well.'
TERRY EAGLETON
ISBN 1-904341-58-6 (pb) £9.99

Kafka
by Klaus Wagenbach
'one of the most useful books on Kafka
ever published.' New Scientist
ISBN 1-904341-01-2 (hb) £12.99
ISBN 1-904341-02-0 (pb) £8.99

Moreschi, The Last Castrato
by Nicholas Clapton
'an immaculately produced and beautifully
illustrated short volume ... Clapton
is excellent on the physical and psychological
effects of castration as experienced
by Moreschi.'
ANDREW GREEN, Classical Music
ISBN 1-904341-77-2 (pb) £9.99

Mosley
by Nigel Jones
'an excellent brief life of Britain's 1930s
Fascist leader ... Jones does manage to get
a more accurate view of Mosley than some
previous, weightier books.'
FRANCIS BECKETT, Jewish Chronicle
ISBN 1-904341-09-8 (pb) £9.99

Nasser
by Anne Alexander
ISBN 1-904341-83-7 (pb) £9.99
Trotsky
by David Renton
ISBN 1-904341-62-4 (pb) £9.99

Trotsky
by David Renton
ISBN 1-904341-62-4 (pb) £9.99